Praise for *Radical Kinship*

Rewilding Christian spirituality: what does this mean? Rachel Wheeler's new book invites us deeply into this question and into the radical kinship of our broadest creaturely relations—precisely at (and as) the center of Christian life. This book's stretch between wide-ranging scholarly engagement and embodied outdoor practices opens a spirituality that reroots us in the life of the world itself. It could not be more timely, more important, more generative.

—Lisa E. Dahill, Miriam Therese Winter Professor of Transformative Leadership and Spirituality and director of the Center for Transformative Spirituality, Hartford International University for Religion and Peace

Radical Kinship is a supremely wise and practical guide to "ecological conversion" for all of us who work in the area of spirituality and long to align our lives with our convictions about Earth's current state of emergency. It is a book I will keep next to my reading chair to pick up whenever I need a nudge toward more integrity in how I share life with all my creature kin in the Earth community.

—Mary Frohlich, RSCJ, professor emerita of spirituality, Catholic Theological Union

Rachel Wheeler has woven together a solid theological foundation for a movement that is rapidly emerging even within the Christian tradition, and the title captures the core of it. With scholarly acumen and relatable storytelling, Wheeler shows how radical kinship is more than a trendy metaphor. Rather, the practice of living in kindred relationship with all other beings is the loom itself that weaves our life together on this planet. Beyond metaphor, beyond stewardship or sustainability, not only does Wheeler draw the threads of wisdom from across disciplines to rewild the Christian story; she also offers practical ways to rewild our daily lives and spiritual practices at a time when nothing is more important.

—Victoria Loorz, author of *Church of the Wild: How Nature Invites Us into the Sacred* and founder of the Center for Wild Spirituality

Reading classic Christian spiritual traditions in light of our current planetary crisis and in conversation with contemporary ecopsychology, ecophilosophy, and ecological knowledge, Rachel Wheeler invites us to reimagine our relationship to our planetary home and embrace the radically interrelated intimacy that humans share with the rest of the Earth community. In this book Wheeler outlines the shape of a "kincentric ecospirituality." This is truly an important book for all who are discerning what and how we are called to be in this new climate for spirituality.

—Timothy Robinson, Alberta and Harold Lunger Associate Professor of Spiritual Resources and Disciplines, Brite Divinity School at Texas Christian University

A spirited, sobering, and ultimately hopeful meditation on how we might live in greater kinship with all of creation. Compelling in its range of ideas, the book's artistry carries through its tone: Wheeler's gentle but urgent voice strikes a chord in our era of anxiety, endangerment, and loss.

—Matthew Wickman, professor of English and associate coordinator of the Faith and Imagination Institute, Brigham Young University; author of *Life to the Whole Being: The Spiritual Memoir of a Literature Professor*

RADICAL KINSHIP

RADICAL KINSHIP

A Christian Ecospirituality

RACHEL WHEELER

FORTRESS PRESS
MINNEAPOLIS

RADICAL KINSHIP
A Christian Ecospirituality

Library of Congress Cataloging-in-Publication Data

Names: Wheeler, Rachel, author.
Title: Radical kinship : a Christian ecospirituality / by Rachel Wheeler.
Description: Minneapolis, Minnesota : Fortress Press, [2024] | Includes bibliographical references and index.
Identifiers: LCCN 2024003139 (print) | LCCN 2024003140 (ebook) | ISBN 9781506487465 (paperback) | ISBN 9781506487472 (ebook)
Subjects: LCSH: Ecotheology. | Spirituality.
Classification: LCC BT695.5 .W535 2024 (print) | LCC BT695.5 (ebook) | DDC 261.8/8--dc23/eng/20240508
LC record available at https://lccn.loc.gov/2024003139
LC ebook record available at https://lccn.loc.gov/2024003140

Cover design: Kristin Miller
Cover image: "The Saint" by Brad Franco, 2017, illustration on paper

Print ISBN: 978-1-5064-8746-5
eBook ISBN: 978-1-5064-8747-2

The more uncertain I have felt about myself,
the more there has grown up in me a feeling of kinship
with all things.

—Carl Gustav Jung, *Memories, Dreams, Reflections*

within the mesh of the web, Himself
woven within it, yet seeing it,
seeing it whole. *Every sorrow and desolation*
He saw, and sorrowed in kinship.

—Denise Levertov, "On a Theme from Julian's Chapter XX"

Our words can be an antidote to human exceptionalism,
to unthinking exploitation, an antidote to loneliness,
an opening to kinship.

—Robin Wall Kimmerer, "Speaking of Nature"

Remember you are of the Earth,
and with the Earth you will be transformed.

—Ash Wednesday Liturgy, Incarnation Monastery
(Berkeley, California)

For my closest kin and dearest companion in all things,
including the rehabilitation of our wild earthling selves,
Winston Walker Wheeler

Contents

Litany of Gratitude

For colleague, historian, and artist Brad Franco and his allowing me to use his art for the cover of this book. His work epitomizes what I mean by this book's content of playfully engaging the wild sacred and sacred wild as kin. *I am grateful!*

For Karen Eifler, whose imagination, kindness, and wit I enjoy and envy so much. An indefatigable champion of my work, professional life, and personal growth, Karen has created numerous opportunities for me to share my work with others. She is truly a sparkling gem of a person and friend. *I am grateful!*

For Lisa Dahill and her exuberant rewilding of Christian spirituality studies and for sharing resources with me early on in my career as a teacher and writer. The path I'm following is more companionably bright because of her and other colleagues' innovative work. *I am grateful!*

For the many colleagues and students who facilitated the creation of this book through conversation, support, and presence. I am fortunate to have lots of opportunities to practice the creativity, courage, curiosity, contemplation, chaos (even!), compassion, and commitment it takes to be present and responsive to, as well as to shape, what is happening in my corner of the world. Deep gratitude to *all* who share this work at the University of Portland, in the Society for the Study of Christian Spirituality, in the Spirituality and Imagination working group facilitated by Matthew Wickman of Brigham Young University, in my faith communities of Saint Andrew Catholic Church and Sophia Christi Catholic Community, and elsewhere. *I am grateful!*

For Emily King, now of University of Notre Dame Press, who supported me as I began my work in ecospirituality and for the spectacular Laura Gifford of Fortress Press, whose generous patience and thoughtful response to my work have been invaluable to me as I developed and completed this project. *I am grateful!*

For Irene Bailey of Temenos Rising and her guidance in forest therapy with my students over the years. The companioning of owls on multiple occasions, seen on two and heard on a third, has been particularly magical, reminding me of and urging me to deeper love of the wisdom, dignity, peace, surprise, and beauty of our creature kin. *I am grateful!*

For students Gina Del Chiaro and Ajahrain Yellowhair, with whom I was working on a research project on intentional communities' sustainability and spirituality practices in the last months of finishing this book; for the Collegium folks who joined my rewilding retreat during that same period; and for Fr. Daniel P. Horan, OFM, and the folks at St. Mary's College with whom I shared ideas from this book and learned so much about practical innovation on campus. The enthusiasm of all these differing groups kept me going. *I am grateful!*

For my dear friend and guide Toni Tortorilla and her goading words of wisdom near the completion of this book ("You're holding the river back!"); for my dear colleague Rebecca Gaudino, on the cusp of life beyond academia, whose companionship and grace have consoled and inspired me during her time at the University of Portland; and for my dear partner, Winston Wheeler, whose loving care makes all I do possible. *I am grateful!*

Introduction

Radical Kinship

In a time of climate change, global warming, biodiversity loss, and toxification of water, soil, and air, Christian spirituality scholars, practitioners, and people of faith must learn to discern new values in a spiritual tradition that says nothing of these specific challenges to our viable human and more-than-human futures. The sharpening of my recognition of the needs evoked by this time emerged from climate activist Greta Thunberg's accusing rhetorical question ("How dare you?!") at the United Nations Climate Action Summit in September 2019. In her speech, Thunberg called out leaders who were (and still are!) too hesitantly implementing changes to address systemic ecological problems. Her claims were poignant and fierce, among them the simple statement "You are failing us."[1]

Thunberg's words ring in my ears as I face members of faith communities when I preach, undergraduate students when I teach, and potential readers as I write. Am I failing them? How dare I not recognize this moment as requiring that I advance solutions and hope for a future, especially from the resources of the Christian spiritual tradition with which I work? How dare I not minimize, challenge, and transform anthropocentric and speciesist views (as well as sexist and racist views) in this tradition that cause, continue to contribute to, and even exacerbate the many crises we experience now? How dare I not seek, maximize, and celebrate geocentric (earth-centered), biocentric (life-centered), ecocentric (home-/biome-centered), and especially kincentric (relationship-centered) values to advance repair of our physical environs, our diverse cultural communities, and even our psychospiritual lives? How dare I not provide a more adequate response to the anxious and grieving members of the communities with whom I work?

This book engages my own experience as a person of faith, a teacher, and a scholar with lots of questions about how best to navigate the difficulties of this time in human history. The book also engages some of the Christian spiritual tradition to underscore the tradition's dimensions that support a hopeful future through rehabilitated affinity with and care for all who share our earthly home. While underscoring those dimensions, I recognize the troubling dimensions of Christianity referenced tellingly in Lynn White Jr.'s provocative essay, "The Historical Roots of Our Ecologic Crisis." In this essay, White argued that Christianity, with its anthropocentric worldview, deserves the most blame for contemporary ecological crises.[2] Other, more recent writers also repeatedly blame Christianity and can be quite harsh in their assessments. When I read such works as these, I find myself in total agreement with them while thinking, "and yet . . ." This book is about that persistent and unsettling "and yet . . ."

Further, even as I absorb such justly harsh criticism from these thinkers, I also observe a metamodern nostalgia for the religious in environmental spaces I occupy. It is as if a vestigial soulful aspect of the participants in these conversations yearns for language to express kinship, participate in ceremony, and utilize other religious means of organizing their experiences and ideas about relating with the more-than-human world—means that are somehow not available to them within a strictly secular, modern worldview. These participants often lapse into what feels exactly to me like prayer and other spiritual practices associated with mainline religious traditions. Guided meditations, aspects of forest bathing or therapy, use of ecopoetry, and new arts and rituals combine to salve a need that religion has ineffectively met. This lapsing helps me understand how attitudes of reverence and acts of devotion remain important across our species and can be configured so that people feel at ease doing them together, regardless of religious or secular beliefs, values, and communities.

To rehabilitate some of the ways Christianity has been thought to promote attitudes leading to ecological degradation, biblical scholars have charted the way into terrain that Christian spirituality scholars might inhabit now.[3] These biblical scholars' discoveries and creations are leading to newfound insight and practice, affirming Earth community more broadly than its human members. To do this work, ecobiblical scholars have devised a hermeneutic (or process of interpretation) that entails beginning with suspicion that most of our texts, sacred or otherwise, because they are products of human culture, espouse a speciesist bias and are anthropocentric. While there may be nothing necessarily wrong with this bias, except when it negatively affects other species (as it usually does), it certainly helps us to note that we operate within it and to consider that other possibilities for thinking and experiencing exist. To work creatively by inquiring as to the roots of this bias and to counter its dominance in our thinking is vital work in many disciplines and many arenas of human activity today.

A second aspect of this form of analysis includes affirming our radical kinship as creaturely interconnectedness, meaning we can use our shared material substance and membership in an Earth community to discern how our actions impact others and vice versa. We may not see all the implications of this interconnectedness, which is one reason that collaborative, transdisciplinary, and interspecies work is so important as we help each other discern what we cannot discern alone. We can also explore and affirm the various meanings that emerge, especially from biblical texts, that demonstrate these interconnected relationships and celebrate our creaturely companionship as God's beloved. Many prophetic passages, for instance, highlight in an ongoing meaningful way, both for readers who espouse a faith commitment and those who do not, the connection between human injustice and environmental damage (see Isaiah and Hosea for examples that resonate with contemporary experience).

Thirdly, by looking beyond our anthropocentric bias we might learn something more wise and more important about our human story from the perspective of other creature kin, we live more fully into our radical kinship. Considering deeply, for example, the reciprocity of relationship between tree and reader of the first psalm of the Hebrew Scriptures could school us in how we, too, sink roots into not only the words of sacred text—what seems to be the psalmist's main preoccupation—but also into the physical environs of our lives, our human and other-than-human communities, and the bioregions that support us. We contribute to each other's lives the way that water and a tree's leaves and fruits give back to the land that supports them. Reading the Bible and the classics of the Christian spiritual tradition through our new and renewed ecological knowledge and awareness of life beyond our human community supports the possibility of our own continued species and our creature kin flourishing amid numerous crises today.

The Catholic geologian Thomas Berry suggested we might throw out the Bible for a time and redirect our meaning-making practices to engage the story of the universe's journey, the emergence of Earth and Earth's own story, the story of life processes on Earth, and the human story. Each of these stories is multifaceted and complex beyond our wildest imagining! Berry may not have had a methodology for this redirecting of our work, and he remained interested in textual cosmologies of various religious traditions throughout his life. However, he certainly valued deep time as a sacred reality and life in community with the red oak, Hudson River, and other Earth community members of his own bioregion as significant means to *reinvent the human*. This pairing of textual study with study of and companionship with the outdoors maps well onto what many of us in Christian spirituality have been trained to do, in part. What remains is to revitalize our engagement with the outdoors, the wild, and the many ways the Spirit manifests in and activates movement through our living world. As we carefully calibrate what to draw forth from biblical texts and the classics of the Christian spiritual tradition, we learn how to effectively set aside less useful texts or to play with them to tease out possibilities that help us transform our current systems and live with more hope in the chaotic present.

More recently, frameworks of biblical interpretation are also being broken open when applied beyond the written text as when, for instance, Leah Penniman, cofounder of Soul Fire Farm in New York, plays with classic strategies to include Earth in her meaning-making strategy. She explains how people of Jewish, Christian, and Muslim faiths have discerned layered meanings within and from their sacred texts. While Islamic readers may look for literal expression, allusion, subtleties, and the deepest realities in the Qu'ran, Christian readers have traditionally looked for literal, allegorical, tropological, and anagogical meanings in their Bible. Significantly, Penniman builds on the Jewish interpretive framework that forms an acronym for the Hebrew word for orchard: *pardes*. She then engages an Earth community member, specifically a rotting log, as she works through what she calls an "earth exegesis."[4] She finds the literal, direct, and surface meaning of the rotting log to require her to look closely at the log and discern signs of transition all over the log's body. A second examination for allegorical, hidden, or symbolic meaning brings *generosity* to mind as she interprets the log's transition as a giving of material for other beings' lives and sustenance. Thirdly, Penniman considers a comparative, temporal, and interpretive meaning in drawing on deep time to understand and experience the rotting log's ancestral, cosmological origins. Finally, experiencing the rotting log's esoteric and mystical meaning leads Penniman to worship and a breaking open of her heart in love and gratitude for the life of this precious part of creation.

To participate in such an ecologically informed engagement with biblical texts and to extend this work into the textual traditions forming Christian spirituality and the broader world that comprises my own personal experience of "nature," I mean to rewild the Christian spiritual tradition, highlighting the ways that *kinship* binds us with one another as members of our Earth community. I do this rewilding work with acknowledgment of and profound respect for the Lutheran ecotheologian and spirituality scholar Lisa Dahill and with admiration of her groundbreaking work of rewilding the field of Christian spirituality. Dahill's rewilding proposal includes specific engagements, encouraging scholar-practitioners to develop and work with ecohermeneutics as described earlier, to address the natural sciences as dialogue partners, and to attend to indigenous wisdom.[5] These are all avenues of exploration that invite and inspire me. I hope they invite and inspire you as well. Similarly, my focus on the Christian desert tradition has been inspired by Douglas Christie's contemplative ecology framework, in which he transposes many virtues and values from early protomonasticism to make sense of his own twenty-first-century experience.[6]

What does it mean, in the context of this book, to rewild as a means to rehabilitate one's identity as kin within a larger field of family relations? Rewilding is a conservation strategy inviting recognition of human limits and adopting human restraint in relation to habits promoting progress and development. In rewilding, humans affirm nature's ability to enact ecological repair, maintenance, and flourishing on nature's own terms, comprised of so many different life-forms and lifeways that may, and often have, apparently competing interests. We are certainly a part of nature, yet rewilding means yielding our power to control these competing interests and becoming cognizant of and living from the very real species vulnerability we have among so many countless other species. Rewilding is an activity that affirms the values and the wisdom of the natural world and of the wild; it also involves figuring out how to balance our human ingenuity and even our own wildness with the way other earthlings live and with greater continuity with the vaster web of life of which we are a part. Wildness can be romanticized as that beyond the reach of humans. Yet an essential feature of living our radical kinship relations means integrating the wild and habitable, experiencing ourselves as a species at home in this world even as we live and act from profound respect for the needs of other creature kin and from our ability to honor the limits to our own capabilities and powers when we sense that our actions harmfully impact others.

While the Christian spiritual tradition is a product of human culture, it was shaped over centuries by people in profound relationship with other wild creatures and phenomena beyond the human: animals, plants, mountains, deserts, rivers, dark nights, and seasonal changes, to name just a few. Even when the wild was thought to be domesticated, in being contained within a person's garden or household, plants and companion animals still retain wildness as a quality of essential unpredictability and liveliness beyond human control. Often our relationships with the wildness that persists around us are mediated through language that can quickly turn metaphorical, replacing the actual living wild beings around us with their theorized, abstracted qualities. This turning of the material into the abstract through our human symbolic consciousness in language and other means of expression is valid, and for those of us schooled in literature, it can be a vital source of play and pleasure. I won't often succeed in wholly loosening myself from attachment to this form of playing with the relationship between words and metaphors and their tie to the physical world. I celebrate the attunement between inner and outer ecologies that this metaphor-making facilitates. To physically rewild, however, can act as an antidote to our doing this metaphorical rewilding unconsciously. To reground in the actual vital, living world we inhabit can be a restorative activity evoking awareness and celebration of our *literal* relationships and kinships—all that makes our lives possible. Renewing our appreciation of how language and metaphor within our various spoken conversations and written discourse connect us with a living community helps us remain open to what is both ancient and new—and crucially needed at this time.

A rewilded Christian ecospiritual tradition emerges as restoration of Christianity's life-generating and life-sustaining norms that express faithfulness to, awe of, and collaboration with the living Spirit who breathes through the sources comprising the Christian tradition. Rewilding work will happen in this book through creative play that weaves together biblical ecospirituality, ecohermeneutical analysis of the so-called classics from the Christian spiritual tradition—most often the Christian desert tradition with which I am most familiar—and concepts gleaned from environmental philosophy, ecopsychology/ecotherapy, and ecopoetics. These last three fields are particularly exciting to me as consisting of disciplines that evoke new meanings and new possibilities for experience, values, lifestyle choices, and commitments for those engaging the classics of Christian spirituality. As is true of other work in the field of Christian spirituality, cultivating radical kinship through rewilding the Christian spiritual tradition is *transdisciplinary* work. Part of this work requires *transcending* typical sources of scholarship, *transgressing* disciplinary boundaries that limit our experience and insight, and *transforming* the work we do to revitalize our engagement with what has always supplemented and yet fundamentally grounded our studies and practices: our own relationships with the living and sacred earth and our creature kin.

For this book, radical kinship names how our ancestors in Christian faith related with one another and with God through awareness and appreciation of the natural world, modeling for us a transdisciplinary engagement with the Bible, other people's stories, and the story of Earth. This transdisciplinary work simultaneously emerges from and cultivates awareness and appreciation that many today are working to revive and celebrate. These ancestors' trust in a radical kinship, whereby their own self-understanding emerged in conversation with the wider and wilder Earth community's members, suggests a means of addressing contemporary issues foreign to them and yet vitally important to us, such as climate change, global warming, species extinction, and pollution. This radical kinship is a kind of creaturely continuity established through the meanings we bring into focus through insisting on a familial relationship with all that is by virtue of our shared material substance and the sacred energies of life that move through and around us.

My weaving of biblical, traditional, and ecological sources is occasioned through the particularity of my own life and stories in conversation with the many wild partners of the natural world that facilitate my being and becoming in a very particular place and with a very particular history. My own literal baptism in the Christian faith took place in the wild, in the form of the Sixes River here in Oregon during a church campout when I was a kid. In my twenties, I committed to being vegan and, later, to living car-free, to not having children, and to adopting other behaviors that draw their significance from my felt contact with and affection for animals, the plant world, and the land. I love language and the arts and studied literature and music before focusing on theology in my graduate studies; my love for the Christian desert tradition emerged in my college years through reading Thomas Merton. My particular story locates me as a writer in the Pacific Northwest of what is now called the United States. I live in what is now known as Portland, Oregon, amid beautiful forests and between two rivers known by many today as the Willamette and Columbia Rivers. I have lived near the ocean and mountains most of my life. I also love the desert wildernesses of this country and the ways they facilitate solitude and attention through intense silences, beautifully subtle monochromatic landscapes, and open, lucid sky. There are deserts, as well, in the eastern parts of this variously fascinating state I live in, and I have camped with students there to engage contemplatively, to learn to pause and listen to voices other than our own. I play the piano, I write poetry, and I knit. My work with the arts opens my being to the creativity I see all around me in the workings of the more-than-human.

My work as a college professor allows me to think with young people about the gravity and opportunities of our moment in time, as a species on the brink of extinction. Many of my life choices made possible by my place and profession enable me to consider, experiment with, and advocate for particular kinship relations. Certainly, this work draws heavily from the intuitions of liberation theology and my desire to build just relationships within the socioeconomic structures we have inherited, relationships that may dismantle and transform these structures. I serve two Catholic faith communities in various ways through liturgical planning and celebration, ecojustice work, and music ministries, even as I grapple with the crumbling of my commitment to the institutional Roman Catholic Church. As a Catholic woman, I deeply admire Pope Francis and the creation care work he champions. I support his vision while also studying and valuing the Earth-based pro-feminine traditions that predate Christianity. Many contemporary concerns in Catholicism feel too parochial in both geography and chronology to encompass the global and historical (into deep time) realities of how people relate to, cherish, and are shaped by their place. This charge of parochialism, however, exists in unresolved tension side by side with my commitment to local communities and their specific members and the places where our religious work—the work of celebrating our bond with the sacred—occurs.

My own family history plays a role in facilitating my awareness of kinship relationships inclusive of and beyond the human. My human kin come from a variety of places, mostly Europe. My childhood and young adult life was peopled with relationships with cats, redwood forests, and the Pacific Ocean. Like many other children, I loved animals, especially the numerous cats who lived with me throughout childhood, into my college years, and now again as a late middle-aged adult: Reba and Sheba, Gracie and Lacy, Franny, Willow, Alyosha, Moth, Samantha, Athena, and Helena. I deeply desire the ability to communicate with not only these cats but also with plants and other creature kin and even places. This is a longing fed, no doubt, by the books featuring human–animal friendships that I read as a child, such as C. S. Lewis's Narnia books and Janette Oke's series of books that adopted the point of view of animals.[7] The anthropomorphism of books like Oke's colored my imagination and made me more open to adopting a critically anthropomorphizing perspective as an adult, aware when I am projecting my own specific form of human experience onto others and desiring to be more sensitive to the ways that animals, plants, and others communicate from experience that is wonderfully strange to and different from my own experience.

My love for creature kin was not always celebrated. In particular, during my teenage years, an adult reproached me for my love of animals, claiming it appeared I loved them more than my human family. That reproach was a deep wound that I have come to see as springing from that person's personal trauma. I have also come to see the reproach as a gift of insight. I *did* claim kinship with animals as important and I continue to do so without shame, even as I understand how our hearts break differently for different reasons when we notice injustice and suffering. I also lean into the experience of being a woman who has chosen not to have children; Donna Haraway's slogan "Make Kin Not Babies!" resonates with me for this reason.[8] As a Catholic woman, it feels important for my exploration of radical kinship that I create and invite possibilities for both lamenting and celebrating people's decisions not to have children. Often this decision allows us to see how reproductive justice might be extended or denied to other species. I work for a world in which women and others wouldn't feel obligated to make the hard decision to not bear children but would feel that living their fertility fully could take lots of different forms, inclusive of but not limited to parenting a child of their own, without peril to so many other creatures' maternity.

Like many others, I long for a life lived in fuller harmony with creature kin all around me and for my work to contribute to and advance solutions for a hopeful future. For that reason, my principal personal and professional interest has become the elaborating of ecospirituality and its constitutive worldviews and practices, as expressed in this book. My working definition of ecospirituality is as follows: ecospirituality describes the experience of relationship with the sacred in the context of *belonging* within our Earth and cosmic homes. Ecospirituality encompasses attitudes and practices that enliven our experience of ourselves as members of the Earth community and that activate our ability to live in a manner expressive of gratitude, respect, care, and joy. Further, to emphasize the belongingness of our human experience evokes home, and who are the ones who typically people our homes? Our family! Our kin! A kincentric ecospirituality explores the many ways that the Earth community we call home makes family a broadly construable concept applied to both human and more-than-human members of the community.

I believe we all, to varying degrees, sense the precipitous moment we inhabit and want to resist the distractions society provides to keep us consuming limited resources and console us on some level for our repressed realization that we are doing so. We find ourselves all too unknowingly complicit in this distraction, keeping us from having the meaningful and satisfyingly transformative lives that I believe we are entitled to while helping the rest of our Earth community members have the meaningful and satisfyingly transformative lives that they, too, are entitled to. This work is offered as a way to think through the implications of the Christian spiritual tradition some of us have inherited and to consider alternatives to its life-destroying implications. As we foster new ways to understand identity, experience, practice, the sacred, loss, love, and vocation at this critical juncture in human history, we contribute to a reweaving of the sacred web of life around us. This work can be done in classrooms and places of worship; in relationships and conversations between spiritual director and directee, students and teachers, and pastors and parishioners; and in personal changes of lifestyle that bring us into richer relationship with our own bodies and the creature kin of our bioregions. I pray, in the words of John O'Donohue, that

> we learn to walk
> Upon the earth
> With all [our animal kins'] confidence
> And clear-eyed stillness
> So that our minds
> Might be baptized
> In the name of the wind
> And the light and the rain.[9]

ECOSPIRITUAL KINSHIP PRACTICE: TRANSFORMING OUR WORK

As scholars of Christian spirituality, we likely spend a lot of time preoccupied with studies and ministries that bring us into contact with texts and other people in professional and indoor spaces: churches, offices, libraries, classrooms, and even our own homes. Our solitary spiritually formative practices like prayer and meditation may also often take place indoors.

Certainly, one strategy to transform our work as scholar-practitioners would be to green or rewild these indoor places by simply bringing the outdoors in. Maybe a few small things already join you in your work—a shell, rock, or pinecone you've picked up during a special vacation. Maybe plants or companion animals are all present with you in the indoors in a way that allows you to be more intentionally engaged as you perform (and play!) as a scholar-practitioner. We might also bring the wild into our physical texts by pressing a few dried flowers between the pages of a favorite book as a keepsake of beauty or to mark a favorite place in the text, read or reflected on in a special outdoor place. Drawing the outdoors in, without harmfully impacting our bioregions, means we rebalance in part the disorienting distinction between inside and outside that so damagingly characterizes modern life. To physically connect with the materiality and the substance of the outdoors within is precious work that grounds our engagement with what may otherwise feel too cerebral, disembodied, and abstract.

We might also consider how reading or engaging with our typical textual sources in the outdoors evokes fresh consciousness of the meaning and purpose of the work we do. Reading aloud outdoors, for instance, evokes consciousness of our being heard by numerous critter others who may or may not take notice of us (great for acquiring the humility to endure the reality that one's scholarship and one's spirituality may go unnoticed!). Reading aloud also allows our bodies to express what our minds take in, to embody meaning while expressing ideas. We might consider: How do the words of our ancestors in faith sound when evoked against the backdrop of a beautiful or a devastated landscape? Do they seem more or less relevant, and if so, how so and why? Turning the sanctuary, office, library carrel, classroom, or study inside out and becoming more proximate with our sacred wild kin is a good way to engage in kinship play.

Further, it's important to be mindful of the materiality of the objects with which we engage—whether indoors or out—the numerous books and screens that contain words and that are made from parts of trees, mountains, oceans, and the earth. Our heightened awareness of how our own creation of scholarship necessarily draws on the resources of our planetary life should help us regard it more fully as sacred work. Every word we compose should be worth the material cost of the energies of life required to share it with others.[10] We might pair this consciousness with knowing our work will ultimately be rewilded itself (often beyond our intention!). Not long ago, I was in a bookstore in Astoria, Oregon, overhearing a conversation between the bookseller and a customer about an author of a local mycology guidebook who planned to spread fungal spores over the pages of a copy of his book in order to grow mushrooms—with which he planned to brew some concoction he might drink, thus eventually literally drinking his own book! For me, overhearing this aspiration gave new meaning to Ezekiel's vision of being told to "eat a scroll" that tasted sweet but settled sourly in his belly (Ezek 3:3). It's valuable to consider the pre- and post-consumption reality of the physical objects of our books, those we study and those we create: the tree pulp, petroleum, minerals, metals, water, wind, sun, and other material parts of creation that enable us to save and share our words for and with one another and the inevitable decline of our work into the material, finite components of our planetary home.

CHAPTER ONE

Kinship Identity

Creativity—Personhood—Transcorporeality

We are the feast.[1]

While it's true that some scholar-practitioners of the Christian spiritual tradition have begun (or have begun again?) to treat human identity as one of shared membership within larger Earth and cosmic communities, we often are still far from realizing this in our everyday lives. Human exceptionalism and anthropocentric bias remain the norm in most cultural circles, those that build upon Christianity especially. After all, Genesis 1 seems to single out humanity as the sole species created in the image of God, and many biblical scholars interpret this first account of the sequence of creation as positing humanity as the pinnacle of creation—not as younger, dependent siblings of other species as many Indigenous cosmologies hold. The second of the Genesis creation stories brings human identity down to earth, so to speak. In describing an anthropomorphized God as planting a garden and then shaping the human form out of the literal earth, the Hebrew text ties the words for human and for earth together as *adam* and *adamah*, respectively. The sensibility expressed in this linguistic link could rehabilitate some of the human exceptionalism embedded within Christianity. Other theologians have also affirmed human animality by way of biblical texts,[2] helping us establish and renew our creaturely continuity with the other-than-human. Both Genesis creation stories together can be seen to work to emphasize humanity's creaturely continuity: with what or whom we regard as divine and what or whom we regard as earthly. And maybe these two categories are not so distinct from one another as might be thought.

Founded on this biblical principle of creaturely continuity, writings in the Christian spiritual tradition routinely feature divine, animal, and vegetal identities as ways to understand the human. Increasingly, our enclosure within houses, schools, places of employment, and even our means of transportation have rendered us ecologically separate from and illiterate about the so-called natural world. Thinking of and with other life-forms can seem incomprehensible to many today. In a way, then, we have returned to the garden—though the garden is now a sterile, artificial enclosure of our own making, filled with our own toys and gadgets. We have returned to the existential loneliness of the Bible's first human, having access to much of what has been engineered to satisfy us, yet lacking a lived experience of our creaturely kinship relations with others. To understand our sacred texts and traditions better, we may have to become aware of and reacquainted with the working of the natural world—of which we are a part—which will allow us to better communicate about, understand, and even experience the world of which these texts speak. This reacquaintance will not only help us understand ourselves better but also result in better and more just relationships with other species!

Central to the genre of spiritual writing and the "classics" in the discipline of Christian spirituality is reflection on questions about human and other-than-human identities, such as Who am I and who are we? What is my and our role, purpose, or meaning in life? Who is God? How do I as a creature relate to Creator and to other creatures? These are perennial questions that spring from a variety of human experiences, especially of pain and pleasure, strife and solace. Principally, perhaps, we experience ourselves as interpreters, as beings who seek and reflect on meaning from our experiences and who tell stories to ourselves and to one another about what has happened and about the meaning of what has happened. For this reason, as scholar-practitioners of Christian spirituality we are acting from an important dimension of our human identity when we are engaged in both our studies and our practices since they involve experiences of presence and meaning-making. These central tasks constituting human identity do not vanish or diminish with rewilding. Rather, the stories we tell and value accrue new meanings for us alongside the new self-understanding they offer us as members of a larger, diverse Earth community. Likewise, such stories help us confirm and even grow this self-understanding.

Understanding human identity, however, is a complicated endeavor, as *we* are the ones attempting to define ourselves. Like the classic koan that describes the impossibility of clapping with one hand, other paradoxes such as biting one's own teeth or seeing one's own eyes illustrate what we are up against when trying to apply our own minds, our own efforts, and our own standards to self-understanding. This essential paradox breaks open, however, when we realize fully our creaturely continuity and sense that the answers to our questions of human identity will be arrived at only through proximity when answering questions about others—answers that are always necessarily incomplete as well—and learning about relationships we have with creature kin that are constitutive of our being. Even so, a primary obstacle to this recognition of creaturely kinship is a misguided sense of our own uniqueness, set apart from everyone else in creation. As we get over this assumption and dwell more fully into our creaturely continuity with all that is, we will be able to reimagine possibilities for our experience, relocate the sacred, and recognize a whole host of other benefits that accrue throughout creation. In a sense, as in the classic conundrum of attempting to define God through apophaticism, or negative theology that explores all that God is by way of all that God is *not*, our habitual sense of ourselves has often used the creaturely other only to help us understand who *we* are *not*. While useful to some degree, our tendency to value uniqueness comes at a psychological and spiritual cost, which some have gone so far as to identify as a cultural narcissism.[3] We could develop a radically kataphatic, or affirmative, approach to defining the human with all we can say about ourselves and other creature kin as members of a vast, diverse Earth community. Celebrating all we have in common will ground us as a species at home in our planetary setting.

ALWAYS BEGINNING

Scientific insights today reveal our genetic proximity to so many other species that kinship is no whimsical metaphor but a living reality with which we must grapple. Indigenous peoples have known of, respected, and celebrated living with *all our relations* as a matter of course for millennia. Even our own bodies, we discover, are teeming with and *are* communities of life, be they bacterial, viral, or some other such microreality. Where "we" as human beings leave off and other beings begin is becoming fuzzier, at best, than we may yet know how to appreciate. Just as Augustine of Hippo classically delineated the Trinity through his self-understanding as triune—he could experience himself simultaneously as knower, known, and knowing; willer, willed, and willing; lover, loved, and loving—so might we begin to understand ourselves and other creatures as multiplicities and as templates for understanding the multifaceted, dynamic, sacred other both within and without, immanent and transcendent.

The Trinity as a Christian theological mystery of divine being and becoming can hardly be picked apart to identify specific persons; each exists as a function of relationality with the others. To pick them apart has constituted heresy in the past even as we might try to make sense of the differing roles each person of the Trinity performs. The consubstantiality—or cobeing—of each part helps Christians understand how other wisdom and scientific traditions feature coemergence as a function of reality. For instance, a parent's identity is formed by virtue of having offspring: the parent and offspring *become* as an essential part of their respective identities in relation to one another, fundamentally, of course, as kin relationships—human or otherwise—but also by virtue of their being energized matter bonded in activities that coform each of them in visceral ways. The person who cares for the young *becomes* the parent in the doing of parenting. This dimension of reality extends to all our collaborative coforming with and of one another.

The Genesis stories of creation present a cosmovision that celebrates diversity across material bodies while also celebrating the continuity that joins them, emergent from Earth as cocreator with God; furthermore, God pronounces all this diversity and emergent continuity "good," an affirmation that can coax our own movement into affirming diversity and continuity as good. Thomas Berry has spoken about basic principles of our universe story that resonate with this God-affirmed diversity and continuity. He named these principles *differentiation*, *subjectivity*, and *communion*, and they facilitate the multiple ways the universe is continuously creative, always (in a sense) beginning and always thus changing. The inner orientation and story that emerge from every specific part of creation add to the magnificent ongoing creativity of the whole. Berry was fond of citing his namesake, Thomas Aquinas, about the impossibility of God's goodness being expressed perfectly by any one part of creation; thus, he posited the necessity of diversity. Even so, the apophatic tradition hints at the excess that divine being still represents in not being fully disclosed by all that has been created and is being created. We might wonder, then, about all that reveals something of the Creator experiencing a diminishment now as the sixth extinction event accelerates and so many species have already disappeared and *are* disappearing. What relationship with the sacred has been and is being curtailed by this ongoing ghosting of species, making God's being increasingly about absence rather than presence? How are we losing vital information about who we are in relation to the divine as we lose these many kin?

The principles Berry elaborated on explain how creative tension between expansion and contraction as an aspect of gravitational powers governed the precise possibilities of coming into being of the universe and the coming into being of life in the universe. He expressed this as a compassionate curvature of tensions that, fractal-like, are scaled from universe to Earth to life to human stories of coming into being and continuing to be in an persistently creative manner that he called *cosmogenesis*. The relationships we have with one another help in this self-fashioning, and the relationships we, as a species, have with other species facilitate our species-fashioning. While origin stories may help anchor our identity as emergent in time and place, offering us a way of sensing ourselves better, the more we use language of our world's ending, with climate change likely to make our planet inhabitable, the more we are caught in a so-called middle, between beginnings and endings. This bookending may not reflect reality as that which is always emergent, always changing, always new. Berry's *cosmogenesis* taps into this dynamic quality of life so that we don't necessarily seek ancient origins but foster awareness of how every time and every place serve as an incubator for new iterations of life and being.

The first creation account in Genesis speaks of all the kinds of creatures that emerged into being, responsive to divine desire. This may appear as an argument against evolutionary science, but the mythic power of this story has more to do with highlighting the diversity of beings that inhabited Earth and cohabited in seeming peace—a vision that later recurs for Isaiah and the prophetic imagination, in contrast to the warring conflicts of humans and the impacts of social injustice on the land. The prophets' visions of the day of the Lord, of God's reign, and of a kingdom of God bespeak a nostalgic return to this utopian Eden. That some of this return might be accomplished militaristically should give us pause. Alternatively, envisioning God's kingdom as a *kindom*, as feminist and mujerista scholars have taught us, aligns well with the transition in our understanding of reality and how we might live within and celebrate familial relationships with one another and all beings.[4]

For some, anticipating a return to paradisal equanimity or Isaiah's vision of a creaturely peace where lions and lambs lie together and humans and snakes are in harmony (Isa 11) bespeaks a misguided nostalgia and denial of the real. Some Christians might believe creation's so-called fallenness is expressed in predatory relationships, literal and metaphorical, that will be reversed in an Eden-like heaven restored to us beyond time and place. Others critical of the unrealism of this vision affirm predatory relationships when they are understood as a function of kinship and coconstituting relations. Nearly the only way most of us with colonized imaginations can imagine predation is of one creature losing out to another's appetite. Other ways of looking at this reality affirm the giving of life to support life, death as a sacred part of the cycle of life, and the consent that is sought and exchanged in communication norms beyond human language and comprehension by species whose predator/prey relationship has occasioned their mutual coevolution and their cobelonging. To disdain this relationship in whole would be to not exist, in that every part of life occasions some feasting on other parts of creation. Without doubt, our military-industrial agricultural complexes are out of alignment with creaturely kinship relationships that are wholesome; instead, animal bodies are routinely prepared for human consumption and subject to human need. This misalignment is damaging our identity as a species that so far seems incapable of living respectfully within kinship relations with others. However, we restore these relationships when we grow aware of the injustice embedded in practices that serve only our own species and we change our ways of being accordingly.

INNER AND OUTER ECOLOGIES: *THE SPIRITUAL MEADOW*

I study the Christian desert tradition, which consists of literature created by and about people living in the late antique deserts of Egypt, Palestine, and Syria. Much of the literature began as oral storytelling about the lifeways of people who were trying to simultaneously rewild and divinize their human identities in contrast to the roles the Roman Empire required them to fill: that of citizen, primarily, and for women, mothers of citizens. To read this literature carefully and in the context of a world so far removed chronologically and (for me, at least) geographically requires cultivating empathy for the situations of Christians already anticipating the endings of worlds, socioeconomic and religious, and living accordingly. In this way, we are kin, as today we live within worlds in transition too. These desert Christians believed that getting close to the land meant getting close to sacred powers, and their habits and lifeways in the desert continue to have lessons for us today. They were reimagining their human identity in the contexts of their worlds, just as today we need to reimagine what it means to be human and to live as kin with our diverse Earth community members. Though the cultural contexts may differ for most of us, a through thread linking the lives of these ancient Christians and our own lives might be discerned in linking our worlds in transition and at the precipice of deep change. Reimagining work invites us to *creativity* as a central facet of our work in Christian spirituality on these edges, as we consider who we actually are and who we want to be, and to identify our discipline or "field" of Christian spirituality and what we want it to be.

One of the desert stories collections has my favorite title: *The Spiritual Meadow*. This book is a collection of stories that the author and narrator, John Moschos, represents himself as finding, much as a wanderer might collect wildflowers in a meadow. "I have called this work *meadow*," he explains, "on account of the delight, the fragrance and the benefit which it will afford those who come across it."[5] The stories' exemplar characters (human and more-than-human) and their acts of Christian asceticism and compassion bloom within the reader's apprehension as varied fragrant wildflowers—the roses, lilies, and violets—of the meadow. Moschos represents himself as having plucked the flowers to weave into a beautiful crown for his reader and yet also represents himself as a "wise bee" gathering nectar from the flowers of the meadow, just as Antony the Great was so represented in his earlier life story written by the Alexandrian bishop, Athanasius.[6] Moschos writes:

> For the virtuous life and habitual piety do not merely consist of studying divinity; not only of thinking on an elevated plain about things as they are here and now. It must also include *the description in writing of the way of life of others.* So I have striven to complete this composition to inform your love, oh child; and as I have put together a copious and accurate collection, so I have emulated the most wise bee, gathering up the spiritually beneficial deeds of the fathers.[7]

This description can be read as corresponding to a recognition voiced by Thomas Berry that we need to shift from a theological focus in the Christian spiritual tradition ("studying divinity") to an anthropological ("gathering up the spiritually beneficial deeds of the fathers") and finally to an ecological ("writing of the way of life of others," human and more-than-human).[8] Each shift elaborates a particular mediation or encounter and builds on the previous, so that now has become our moment to comprehensively engage the sacred, the human other, and all creation in our theological reflection and our spiritual practice. While understanding differentiation as useful to distinguish these various elements of our human life, we may also foster the capacity to understand and feel the resonance between them. Consider rereading the excerpt from the preface to *The Spiritual Meadow* and hear how it's possible to read "writing of the way of life of others" as an invitation to study not only Scripture and one's experience of God through "habitual piety," for instance, but also written texts like nature writing; other disciplines like biology, geology, chemistry, and physics; and other "texts" like the so-called natural world. Certainly, Moschos likely meant human others, those he terms spiritual "fathers," yet acknowledging his (and our) anthropocentric bias, we might creatively expand this invitation to include the ways of life of more-than-human kin as well. That Moschos's own work routinely mentions these creature kin means they may also constitute the exemplarity he wishes to offer his readers.

Staying with *The Spiritual Meadow*, we might read just the first couple of stories to exemplify what their rewilding entails and thus reveals—what happens when we look beyond the stories' anthropocentric bias and consider the more-than-human exemplars within them and thus a way to rethink the human as a species with parents amid many other creature kin beyond our own species. The first story is about a holy man desiring to visit Mount Sinai. Significantly, he is about to be appointed leader of a monastic community and doesn't seem to relish this opportunity (a typical situation among the so-called desert fathers). Instead, he departs for Mount Sinai but hardly gets underway on his journey before he becomes sick and takes refuge in a nearby cave. There he stays for several days and through his fevered delirium has visions of John the Baptist. Note there is a *river* that the man has crossed on his truncated journey, there is a *cave* that he interprets as offering refuge, and there is a *mountain* of desire—all features of the landscape facilitating this person's identity through traveling toward an alluring mountain that initiates the journey, then through becoming sick, and then through being restored to health in a cave.

When John the Baptist appears to the feverish holy man, John tells him that he needn't go all the way to Mount Sinai, for "this little cave is greater than Mount Sinai."[9] And though initially resistant to this invitation to stay, once the holy man agrees, he is instantly healed. He subsequently builds a church in the cave—sacralizing what we can regard as already a sacred refuge—and many come to join him. The story's connecting of place and person happens through biblical exemplars: Moses is associated with Mount Sinai, John the Baptist with the River Jordan, and the prophet Elijah with a place within which he took refuge during drought—all weaving this particular holy man's identity and story within others' stories and within particular places. Even his body's fever schooled his mind in its desire to go to a remote holy setting and instead to recognize through visionary experience the sacred quality of a place already present to him. Note also that he didn't return to the community where he was supposed to have become a leader. Instead, he seems to have recognized a vocation to build community in the place en route to his supposed destination where he found refuge. Just as such a man's story might show us a way to be present in our places and not wish to be otherwhere, so might we think about our experiences with aspects of our home landscapes and how they have shaped our identities and our stories, delimiting our desired movements while also offering vocation, as much as our human family members and friends have shaped us. This story speaks to my own age-old desire to found a farm sanctuary for animals and a hermitage for rewilding human identity beyond our cityscapes. It reminds me of the delightful vocation of simply rewilding my own homestead in the urban neighborhood where I live—the particular set of four apple trees, a pear tree, a fig tree, the resident outdoor cats and squirrels, the insects, the blue jays, and the starlings all rely on me in some way to live in a manner conducive to their ongoing flourishing.

The second story in *The Spiritual Meadow* is brief—as is typical of many stories in these collections making up the literature of the Christian desert tradition. It reports simply: "There was another elder at that place . . . whose virtue was so great that he would welcome the lions which came into his cave and feed them at his lap, so full of divine grace was this man."[10] The sanctity of the desert dwellers is often manifested in peaceful interspecies relations like this one. The lions in this story communicate their recognition of the man's holiness through their accepting his companionship in their domain and even receiving food from him. That Moschos attributes this to the man's being "full of divine grace" is telling and evokes our own possibilities of such attribution. Might Jane Goodall's ability to be peacefully among chimpanzees, to be accepted in their domain, be considered evidence also of *sanctity*? Her stories tell of the disciplined patience it took to acquire that acceptability—something we may need to be reminded of when we consider our own capacity as human beings and what we define as holy. Some interspecies relationships may come more naturally to us than others—those with pets, for instance, who live with us in our homes. Most, however, require the patient and resolute rewilding of our own lives to match the needs of wild others.

These desert stories are good resources for helping us imagine what, in fact, constitutes a virtuous life and what sanctity looks like. I wonder what this second story might sound like if imagined from the lions' perspective. Might the lions as subjects in a story and lifeworld of their own reveal something important to us? What would lion kinfolk think of their ancestors in these stories? Would they ridicule them for trusting a human, given what many interspecies relations look like today? What genre of writing might this constitute for an animal reader: horror, comedy, romance? Could this kind of consideration also move us to better relationships with our animal kin? I'd like to imagine, perhaps in my own species' interest, that it might indeed be counted sanctity among lionfolk for lions to live in communion with a human and to find food at their hands—not, in fact, to find the human body itself their source of food. To exercise some kind of their own restraint. Is this unrealistic—as in the biblical peaceable kindom motif reflected on earlier—or is this an *interspecies asceticism* that is just as exemplary for the readers of John Moschos's *Spiritual Meadow* as other examples of human ascetic feats might be? That the lions let the man live peaceably in a cave registers another fact of human experience for us: creaturely authority lies often with our creature kin and beyond our volition. If we don't cultivate good, balanced relations with this kin, we simply won't survive. Not only does this story, then, express the exemplary in terms of sacred living (what typically constitutes virtue and holiness), but it also opens up this sacredness to our consideration of the biological. Living in balance, making sure each species has the food its members need, is an important quality and even an identifying marker of our human identity that we, as well as other species, have agency over. Francis of Assisi and the wolf of Gubbio later depict this communal reciprocity of care. We are meant not just to marvel at the power of humans to pacify animals who may naturally be a source of terror for the humans but also to recalibrate our sense of creaturely continuity to understand that other species have their needs, which we must appreciate and respect.

A TRANSCORPOREAL ECOSPIRITUALITY

I purposely use *reimagining* to describe the work we might do to rewild our identities in relation to our obligations to creature kin today and to the work of engaging our scholarship and practices to support that rewilding. Thomas Berry has used the idea of *reinventing*, and while I appreciate the specific components of his proposal and will detail them briefly, I also register the mechanistic quality of this naming. For me, *invention* is a word to be associated with tools, manufacturing, and our own products, rather than the creaturely creativity with which we were born. To reflect that mechanistic, skill-based, learned quality of our human activity on our own species doesn't feel like quite the right name. Nevertheless, Berry described one component of what he called "the great work"[11] of our time as creating "a new language, even a new sense of what it is to be human."[12] It is this acquiring and even creating a new sense of ourselves that Berry's invitation spells out that I most want to focus on. Such a sense comes from our experienced, embodied reality as creature kin.

Some of the reinventing Berry proposes will sound familiar to those whose sensibility and worldviews have been shaped within Earth-based spiritualities, but for many of us this reinventing constitutes a radical new self-appraisal. We may need to adopt behaviors that are quite different from behaviors to which we likely feel entitled and which we feel to be natural, both in and of themselves and as part of our social milieu. This adoption of new behaviors could be precipitated by awareness of trauma, our own or others'. Reflecting on the wildfires in Australia that destroyed so much habitat and wild lives, for instance, Australian ecophilosopher Freya Mathews described the changes to her identity that living in relationship with these creature kin required of her:

> I now have no choice but to disengage materially from my civilization to a degree it had not before been possible even to contemplate. There must be no more air travel; I must give up driving; food must be thoroughly ethically sourced; I must rid my life of

> plastic; any further commodities or clothes I may require must be purchased second hand. When all this has been negotiated, I may again take stock, and consider what further agents of death my manner of living is unleashing on my kin.[13]

Further, Mathews avers that "whatever consequences such personal reforms entail for my social identity—my identity as a respectable professional and member of society—is no longer the issue. If I emerge from the process shabbier, gap-toothed, less professionally available and less presentable, so be it."[14] Mathews's reflection highlights the constitutive dimensions of the koala's identity in particular as one species severely impacted by the wildfires in 2019. Responsiveness to loss and devastations of life resulted in Mathews's adoption of a new identity for herself that impresses me deeply. I fear we are not yet explicit enough about the radical lifestyle changes we know we need to make and are attempting to make. This deferral may be because we want to know the one right thing to do rather than be willing to try. Mathews's willingness to "again take stock" evokes the provisional nature of all our undertakings as reimagining our human identity. Certainly, some of us are still in the near years of such calamities as wildfires, and whatever resolutions they spawn now may be revised in upcoming years. What feels important to me, though, is the willingness to be substantively changed by realizations that our lives today are not working well when they impact others so grievously. Many of Mathews's resolutions have to do with consumption practices and the materials that surround and enable her life. While we may wonder to what degree any of us can really disengage materially, Mathews's resolutions reveal the substance and the material transformation that will be occasioned by changes in habit—as a matter of *transcorporeality.* Hers is a particularly good example of how we might concretely engage Berry's notion of reinventing the human and imagine possibilities for our own contexts.

While Berry's notion of reinventing is presciently metamodern in moving past both overreliance on scientific objectivity and the cynical apathy associated with postmodernity to claim that this new human is not so new after all, living into this newness will be challenging. Indeed, the figure of the reinvented human as an integral ecologist resonates with claims made by Pope Francis in his 2015 encyclical, *Laudato Si'*. We all are invited to become integral ecologists, persons whose relationships with the so-called natural world are facilitated through presence and empathic understanding as we combine scientific knowledge with other ways of knowing from our symbolic consciousness that we typically associate with the humanities.

Berry's invitation for reinventing the human first contains a diagnosis of the Anthropocene and a claim for adjudicating our human engagements. He claims that the present human situation can be described in three simple, declarative sentences: "In the twentieth [and twenty-first] century the glory of the human has become the desolation of Earth. The desolation of Earth is becoming the destiny of the human. All human institutions, professions, programs, and activities must now be judged primarily by the extent to which they inhibit, ignore, or foster a mutually enhancing human-Earth relationship."[15] Berry then continues to define and provide commentary on each element of what he calls the reinvented human: "In the light of these statements, it is proposed that the historical mission of our times is: To reinvent the human at the species level with critical reflection within the community of life systems in a time-developmental context by means of story and shared dream experience."[16] Berry's statement is contained in the appendix to his *The Christian Future and the Fate of Earth*, published in 2009, the year of Berry's death. The statement is an important crystallization of his life's work and expresses the wisdom he learned from studying and writing about cosmology, cultural evolution, and histories of religions. He advocated our leaning into the cosmocentric dimensions of our species identity—that we are *earthlings* and our material bodies are composed of elements that originated within stellar transformations eons ago. We are participatory dimensions of our planetary habitat; our stories and dreams facilitate ongoing creativity, and we should thus be attentive and responsive to them. While our technologies may distract us from our fundamental connectedness with all that is, we must retrain our attention, our industry, our governing principles, our ethics, and our spiritualities to the flourishing of the whole Earth family.

Much of what Berry advocates provides an antidote to the state of the human condition in which we find ourselves in the early twenty-first century. Human vulnerabilities foster fear of the present and the future. We repress rather than acknowledge our persistent ecoanxiety as grief for species and habitat loss, guilt over complicity in this situation, and seeming paralysis in effecting change take over our minds, wills, and hearts. Politics, economics, law, health care, and education are all strategies for human engagement to respond meaningfully to the consequences of inequitable power sharing but are not effective enough when undermined by their constitutive dimensions of patriarchy, racism, and anthropocentrism. To rewild Berry's reinvention of the human means taking this work further, not only celebrating our cosmocentric identity as a species but also considering all the ways that Earth has contributed to our being and all the threads in the web that allow us to find our place here while holding space for other species. This work of simultaneously living within our niche and fostering others' flourishing in their niches as a collaborative enterprise, undoing distinctions between wild and domestic and urban and rural, helps us see how the dynamism of our reality in the twenty-first century requires new imaginings and new practices to continue. When Berry claims that we need "something beyond existing tradition to bring us back to the most fundamental aspect of the human"[17]—this most fundamental aspect being our ability to self-fashion, perhaps—we also have to extend this something to what enables us to celebrate the mutual fashioning of ourselves and our creature kin. While we may still sense there is a uniqueness to our species ability to be deliberate about who/what we want to become that we don't know for sure other species share, a basic self-constitutive feature of our human bodies, minds, and spirits is our engagement with the more-than-human. Without that engagement, none of us would be the beings we are, nor would our species be the species it is. And, reciprocally, many other species would not now be who they are without having interacted with us . . . often for the worse.

We commonly speak of identity crisis as we maneuver through moments that challenge our self-understanding and assumptions about our place in the world. Whether identity crisis emerges in young adulthood as vocational options open or close before us or through loss of financial stability or health or even just the movement into older age, all these moments may feel as if they gently beckon, *or* disruptively force, us into identities we had not previously imagined or wished for ourselves. These moments suggest the ultimate dynamism of life in which the stability of our subjectivity is always necessarily albeit uncomfortably undermined; living into that reality constitutes a meaningful spiritual reconfiguration of our spiritual maturity.

Currently, we are enduring and causing our own species-wide identity crisis as we learn more about the world around us and our impact within this world. We have learned that we are a lot more influential than we perhaps realized was possible as we name this era the Anthropocene, an influence we learned about only a relatively very short time ago! We are also learning how vulnerable we are as our essential being is tied up with our planetary home, which we are (it seems) so casually devastating. The ecological self with which we are invited by many deep ecologists to identify means understanding ourselves as more interwoven within this world than we likely could have imagined or allowed ourselves to feel even just decades ago. This ecological self is one that enables us to recognize, affirm, and celebrate the subjectivity and personhood of so many Earth others with whom we share this planet and to loosen our attachment to the structures and institutions we have built that separate us from the many Earth others with whom we share this planet. To remind ourselves of our own identities, we are having to be mindful again of what more-than-human others teach us. They are not only our spiritual teachers but also our models for how to be human, how to be a creature alive in this world, how to be in relation, and how to experience change as a fundamental axiom of our living and our dying.

I imagine some of the work we have to do to reinvent or reimagine our identity looks like the following. Right now our species awareness is heightened by understanding our destructive impact on our creature kin. Although a great deal is asked of us by the growing existential threats associated with climate change to get to a place of "do no harm" and simple sustainability, even more is asked of us to move beyond that point—insufficient and unsatisfying in the long run—to a place of mutual *flourishing*. However difficult the changed self-understandings and practical actions that we undertake to achieve these movements are, we can be encouraged and motivated in considering two things. First, we already know the intricately bound relationship between our species' consumerism and the impact our extractive behaviors has on the world around us. Second, this knowledge helps us to see that, although our severance from others is a painful, traumatic dimension of our identities, a reversal may be our richest satisfaction and pleasure, not to mention healing, as we imagine and act our identities as Earth community members.

Rewilding Berry's reinvention of the human enables us to consider and experience our identity in relation to the larger and other powers that exist throughout the universe, galaxy, our home planet, and even our biotic communities on Earth. We have options for our mutual self-fashioning. Many of us choose to let our institutions and the technologies that we have made have such authority that they form us. The digital storytelling we engage in as we binge television series or video games makes us into a particular kind of human being that confirms our separation from creature kin—we discern how such living normalizes our inattention to our wider Earth community and its members impacted by our entrancement with our own products. The material extraction and energy use to which so many of our online technologies are directed have left and are leaving a massive imprint on Earth that is part of the devastation our own and other species are experiencing. The rewilded human being lives in a way that again facilitates the mutual beneficent fashioning of self and other within the Earth community. Sustaining local connections, we share resources; we travel, play, and learn together—optimally outdoors—so that just as our human community family members contribute to each other's transforming, we grow and change, flourishing alongside the flourishing more-than-human.

Our predicament emerges primarily from an error related to human exceptionalism, a concept that relates to our thinking of ourselves as not only superior to other creature kin but somehow also as exempt from the consequences of our behaviors in this world. A focus on transcendence, for instance, in the Christian tradition and a focus on hoped-for realities emergent elsewhere—not here on Earth—mean some of us think of ourselves as not beholden to creature kin or expected to bear the brunt of the devastation we've wrought in this particular Earth community. God has, some think, singled us out as a species deserving of a flourishing life here, and if it has been necessary to use (up) all the available resources without special regard for the ways this thinking and acting impact others, then so be it. Only slowly are we coming to realize that such thinking and acting result in compromised ways of life for others and an unfeasible existence even for ourselves. We shouldn't perhaps be surprised at the slowness of this realization. Though such a realization may be buried deep in our consciousness, I think we sense how deeply disruptive our coming to full realization of our negative impact on the so-called natural world will be. Owning our power and allowing ourselves to fully feel the gravity of the impacts of our mistakes should simultaneously prepare us to work together better and to share and even assume more of the burden that others, marginalized humans and the more-than-human, are carrying. There are nevertheless aspects of our species identity that might be worth revaluing insofar as they enable us to grow more critical and cautious about the ways of life we have inherited in the twenty-first century and to grow more creative about imagining alternatives to destructive default ways of life.

These aspects of our species identity are intelligence, insight, intuition, improvisation, and imagination. Though not unique to our species identity, the way we understand ourselves as living these dimensions of human life may be informed by how other creature kin model these dimensions through their own lifeways. We thus adapt and create as we live more fully into our species identity as creature kin mutually fashioning and fashioned by others. This material continuity, which is a constitutive dimension of our being creature kin, evokes a transcorporeal ecospirituality. Drawing on Stacy Alaimo's work on transcorporeality,[18] transcorporeal ecospirituality is the material and formal creaturely continuity we share as a species with all creature kin, by virtue of the flows of substance and energy that comprise our own bodies and the bodies of all who make up our planetary existence. Importantly, Alaimo registers the ways that toxicity and pollution persist across these domains, transforming the dimensions of our "organic" existence and calling into question notions of "purity." I attend to the constitutive elements of a transcorporeal ecospirituality through naming intelligence, insight, intuition, improvisation, and imagination as capacities we need to grow to cultivate kin relationships.

To begin, *intelligence* names a capacity of mind—however located in a body—to organize information and respond to dimensions of life with some degree of understanding the implications of what one encounters. At this moment in our human history, we are puzzling over the multiple ways intelligence manifests, whether as what we now know as *artificial* intelligence (which may be neither artificial nor intelligence!) or as the ways other creature kin create and manifest knowledge. The ways that creatures like insects, birds, and fish move together in a way that facilitates decisions made at a level of intelligent comprehension beyond an individual participant's knowing (or brain) resonates with the ways that our own communities and our bodies-as-communities manifest knowledge. We talk often today of the ways our bodies store and express memories, information, emotion, and trauma as an intelligence that far exceeds what we associate with just our own brain function. Further, the notion of a psyche beyond the human, shared as an *anima mundi* or planetary intelligence or metabolism, that manifests in relationships between different species and different places reminds us of all we have yet to discover and enjoy about the ways that "mind" and intelligence may be transfigured in light of information we need to move responsibly through this traumatizing century.

Deep ecologists such as Arne Ness, Aldo Leopold, John Seed, and Joanna Macy talk about "thinking like a mountain," which though a puzzling and confounding phrase for many, evokes this intelligence that lies beyond our own but somehow invites our own response. What might it feel like to think like a mountain, river, cat, or sequoia? How does our ability to even ask these questions evoke a species identity marker that disrupts our human exceptionalism and enables empathic response? I imagine our hesitancy over thinking it possible to "think like a mountain" may come of our fear of what we might discover if we did. As a hypothetical, could the thinking of our creaturely kin be largely indifferent or hostile to us? Could this other host of beings living among, within, and even *as* us be so saturated in the suffering we cause that no good can be affirmed of our species, which has centered its own projects and pleasures for so much of our human history? It's hard for me even to write of this because I'm convinced other creaturely thinking is so different than anything I can present as a hypothetical here. The manifestation of intelligence in life-forms and in even the inanimate that we typically consider incapable of thought—at least, as we know and regard it—still has a lot to teach us about the potential of using our own human intelligence in new ways. Just as a mountain might think in scales of centuries or millennia and might regard the passage of weather, the growing of trees, and the lifeways of resident mountain creatures all with a deep equanimity reaching into the roots of the earth, so might we as humans learn to think in larger generational spans of time and even to think *patiently*. As a mountain's thought began with the thrusting movement upward through the earth's crust, with magma flowing and pooling in different places on emergent Earth, so might we recognize our own intelligence as emergent within the deep fractures of Earth and Earth community that we are causing. A transcorporeal intelligence refers to the way thinking consists as an emergent activity across shared bodies and minds. Thinking like a mountain, then, may become thinking as a mountain when we recognize our essential transcorporeal, creaturely continuity with the lands we inhabit.

Such thinking may help information about our species and our impacts on Earth community now become *insight*. Insight often has to do with shaping our information into understanding the significance of the information. And though within the word *insight* we hear resonance with only one of our sense acuities, the word can also indicate the way understanding is achieved through various sensual intelligences. Information we're aware of through seeing, hearing, smelling, tasting, and touching allows us to combine the threads uniting different facets of the world with insight—and even wisdom—about our current situation. Transcorporeal insight means attesting to the ways we perceive our own life-form in continuity with other creature kin. I wonder sometimes about the insight my creature kin have about me that I don't have access to myself. An early exercise with my first spiritual director invited me to develop a relationship with a tree on the grounds of Saint John's Abbey, where I was studying at the time, and to grow conscious of being seen and experienced by this other life-form. What/whom did the tree see in seeing me? To consider one's identity and lifeway through the provisional perception of the other-than-human is a curious spiritual practice and, for me, evoked possibilities incipient in my consciousness and not given expression or attention in my formal schooling. Considering the tree's—or any other being's—insight more broadly helps us locate the movement of information and intelligence through various species when, for instance, we think of a tree's perception. As I walk in the local park or sit under the pear tree in the backyard where I live, what insight does the tree have about life in this particular place? What wisdom about me does the tree's perception yield? What insight about seasonal change does the tree manifest when perceiving when to let loose its leaves in the fall? What insight about harmful human behaviors do hurricanes and forest fires express? Learning from these elements of our earthly home, we might consider our own capacity for insight to hone our powers of perception and to change our behaviors that are harmful.

Another aspect of our creaturely continuity with other creature kin is *intuition*, which is akin to instinct. While some humans have historically drawn a firm line between animal instinct and human intelligence—the latter often manifesting as holding one's animal instincts in check through rational thought—I believe a recovery of sacred regard for our powers of intuition is an important ingredient in rewilding and reimagining our human identity. The ability to respond to intuition and even enhance its felt movement in our lives requires that we recognize intelligence in other areas of our bodies. For example, we should give voice to our gut disturbance—a quality of human life in our century, as the food we consume nourishes us so badly—and listen to how our bodies signal important information to us in ways we may not be able to explain. Many intuitions emerge spontaneously and surprise the person who "has" them. They seem to come as qualities of our creaturely lives, open to whomever may have the time to await them and then give them expression. Deeply regarding intuition as a means to identify how we may rewild our human identity in the remainder of this century requires cultivating contemplative capacities, long a staple of human identity and practice in Christian and other religious traditions. Intuition may be encountered as the voice of the divine, of the sacred sounding beyond expectation in our felt hunch to do or say something, though we know not why.

The registering of something that moves us beyond our own knowing is also an important opening to living with mysterious creature kin. An intuition to touch or not touch, for instance, requires us to seek consent with the other. An intuition that some relationships with poisonous plants or unstable ground or a diseased animal may be hazardous requires that we move cautiously in the world. I sense that intuiting the deep uneasiness some of us feel in our jobs may give rise to an emergent freedom, intuiting there is another kind of life that is closer to the land, to our creature kin, and to their wildly unknown lifeways that would deeply satisfy us, provide a deeper pleasure in our lives than we have individually and without the support of human others. Transcorporeal intuition, then, enables us to trust ourselves and our creature kin more fully, without devolving into habits of analysis and explication requiring rationality. Acting on this kind of intuition and even the shared storytelling and dreaming that Thomas Berry's reinvention of the human entailed leads to another important identity marker of the human (though also not unique to the human): *improvisation.*

While creativity about our lives is crucial, many of us may feel this capacity atrophied at best, as our schooling formalizes our complicity in the status quo and prepares us for jobs that incorporate us (embody us) into the workings of the capitalist economy. Through creation of debt, in particular, we grow to imagine we have little choice about how we might live our lives. Being able to imagine alternatives has always been threatening to the status quo and is why the arts are such a vital means of expressing and embodying resistance. Improvisation is playing, acting on our creativity, being willing to make mistakes, being willing to experiment with what's possible until we find we are able to do what we formerly thought impossible. Even our play or improvisation at identity can be important work at this time as we play at being a rewilded being so that we begin to understand what that feels and looks like and begin to model this for one another. This morning, for instance, I was drawn to relieving myself in the backyard as has been my habit on land in more wild places. My relationship with the yard surrounding a home I rent in Portland has been a tentative and resonating romance. While I love the creatures who make their home there, the monoculture of the yard grasses in lawn has signaled to me an increasing blandness of my life, vocationally and spiritually, and the call from the yard to rehabilitate in rewilding has also been felt as a call within myself. Not knowing where and how to start, experimentation has been key. Contributing my life fluids to the undernourished soil is an important improvisation to make on this particular day, not only making a connection with the land but also concomitantly training myself in being responsive to intuitions, letting go of disciplined domesticity and commitment to rationality to try out something else.

I imagine many more of us will need to do this kind of work in our personal and professional lives moving forward, and to give ourselves and each other the kind of grace that will enable us to both laugh at mistakes and take more seriously the devastating effects of *not* fostering our creativity. Just as I admire Freya Mathews's willingness to become shabby in her improvisational response to forest fires in her native Australia, I'm growing increasingly appreciative of the invitation of the Gesturing Towards Decolonial Futures collective to become familiar with ourselves as both "cute and pathetic."[19] Our improvisational attempts to reactivate our lives as creature kin may look messy, offend others, and exclude some, but growing sensitive to that reality while being persistent with what Earth urges us to do through our intelligence, imagining, and intuitions is important work. Our transcorporeal improvisation will allow us to accept the fact that—and celebrate how—our bodies change over time, welcoming the dynamism explicit through our animated being that renders us often unknown wholly to ourselves.

Finally, our imaginations are so important to this work of rewilding and of living with our creature kin. Our ability to empathically identify with the plight of poisoned waters, birds and marine animals consuming plastics, the loneliness of individuals without a mate with whom to endure the ending of their species identity, the parched forest homes overexposed through fires require our imagination to give rise to emotion and activity on behalf of creature kin whose habitat and lifeways have been compromised by our essential *failure* to imagine. A redeemed and rewilded imagination does not impose human qualities on other forms of life but registers from a felt sense of creature kinship and creaturely continuity the possibilities for shared experience that reflect other possibilities for our own being. Transcorporeal imagination moves into species-identifying play even as we encounter others whose imagined inner and outer lives illuminate new facets of sacred mystery.

The ecofeminist philosopher Val Plumwood discovered her mortality in an encounter with a crocodile. Her encounter was a near-death experience in being in a death-roll with the crocodile three times. She lived to tell about it, and the event reshaped her life in significant ways. In the main, she discovered her primal human identity as *prey* and puzzled over the consternation such a discovery occasioned for her, one that she enlarged as constitutive of our species-wide discovery of our vulnerability in regard to the climate chaos we are creating: pollution, forest fires, hurricanes, drought/flood, and more. Plumwood's self-understanding as one entitled to eat and yet not be eaten was undermined by this unusual event that crystallized what was true all the time of her individually and of us as a species. The very naturalness of our being prey—that a crocodile would want and even need to eat us and that others consume us daily and after death is a reckoning most of us would consider morbid in the extreme. Plumwood experienced herself as no more than a feast—all that she valued about her own existence and that other humans might value about her being was nothing when compared to the crocodile's power to make real, to act upon, the crocodile's legitimate need to eat.

A sacrament of Christian communal spiritual experience is the celebration of the Eucharist, when Jesus's body and blood are consumed. The Christian community is in this celebratory act made predatory and nourished, reminded how their own bodies are transformed by the body and blood consumed, becoming what they eat—that is, prey as well as predator. We may not favor thinking of ourselves in this way. Doing so may disturb and dismay. Yet a fundamental reconfiguration of our relationships with others relies on our acceptance of fitting into the whole as a piece that is simultaneously eater and eaten. This cycle occurs every day as we eat our own meals that may (but needn't) be less sacramental in nature than the Eucharist and just as significant in forming us. Similarly, we are the eaten; we are the feast to so many microorganisms who make their homes within and on us, transforming us even as they consume us. We honor these beings by taking care of our bodies.

Earth care can, then, entail care of the little pieces of Earth that our own bodies comprise.

The transcorporeal element to all this is the creaturely continuity we experience with the more-than-human world, with all that is not made by the human but has been created by powers other than ourselves just as we were created by them. Together, we shape each other, and the Anthropocene becomes a name for the power of our humanity to shape planetary life and awakens us to the power we have for mutual flourishing. Donna Haraway points out that though naming our era the Anthropocene can be hubristic when we fail to realize that the planet was transformed by bacteria and then by plant life eons ago, we can take our place in joining the mutually constitutive work of creation. Just as these other-than-human life-forms had and have radically effective relations with shaping the geological, chemical, and biological processes of Earth realities, so have we humans. Catalyzing these powers for the good of ongoing life will constitute our most effective living into our species identity as kin. Octavio Paz's incantatory poem "Wind, Water, Stone" gives shape to the mutually constitutive relationships of these elements of creation. We might adapt such a poem and the transcorporeal wisdom it expresses to encourage our own species to understand the radically connected manner in which we live with others—the landscapes that form us, the animal kin who companion and befriend us, and the waters and winds that compose, refresh, and animate our living bodies.

> Water hollows stone,
> wind scatters water,
> stone stops the wind.
> Water, wind, stone.
>
> Wind carves stone,
> stone's a cup of water,
> water escapes and is wind.
> Stone, wind, water.

Wind sings in its whirling,
water murmurs going by,
unmoving stone keeps still.
Wind, water, stone.

Each is another and no other:
crossing and vanishing
through their empty names:
water, stone, wind.[20]

ECOSPIRITUAL KINSHIP PRACTICE: STAGED CONTINUITY

Our language often reveals an implicit sense of our kinship with other parts of creation. For instance, recently I was reading a poem with students in a desert spirituality class in which the poet uses the word *talus*.[21] I was unfamiliar with the word so had looked it up before class, and I was glad I did because we all agreed we hadn't recognized the word. One student said she felt she *should* know it since she had taken an anatomy class, but we all agreed it was helpful to know it because it reinforced how we interpreted the poet's desire to look for differences amid seeming similarities between the poet's self and the (desert) landscape.

Talus describes a part of the ankle and a sloped part of the landscape near the *foot* of a hill or cliff. A word for a body part joins with naming a feature of the landscape. Of course, this is true of other words such as a *limb* or *trunk* for a tree and human. We talk of bodies of water, as we and other animals have bodies. We certainly also use plant names and other names for features of the natural world for human identities, such as Rose, Daisy, Iris, River, and Sky. What a gift to give a child the implicit recognition of kinship with other parts of creation through a name! Indigenous peoples have known and used the practice of identifying humans with other parts of creation for millennia, and to do so has afforded an understanding drawn from a deep awareness of interconnectedness from which many of us today are estranged.

To consider identity within the framework of kinship and play, we might push our language to reflect understanding of the universe and life expressed through our individual and collective selves by turning our somewhat static names into verbs. What, for instance, would it mean for me to think of myself even occasionally as the universe *racheling* in me? For some, this move might feel too destabilizing of identity and even dangerously so. Marginalized peoples deprived of opportunities to develop a sense of selfhood may need other processes by which to facilitate a sense of identity with others with minimal loss to the self they are and need access to.

My own sense of identity has been so shaped by the patriarchal culture within which I was raised and to which I (unwittingly) contribute that it can be a relief and delight to consider this *racheling* as a setting aside of everything placed on me or adopted by me that keeps me from expressing the being I am. It is also a recognition that something else that helps me shake these obstacles loose persists. This something else is a perennial invitation.

The kinship practice of staged continuity is a strategy for a transforming Christian spirituality that asks the practitioner (you) to get outdoors and explore a bit to embody your kinship through play with others in your natural setting. Find a place where there are other wild creatures with whom you can practice enhancing your sense of our creaturely continuity and dwell for a bit. You might even consider documenting this continuity with a picture, if you use your own body to mark it. Getting close to something other, such as the ground or leaves or a tree's trunk, put your hand or another body part near the aspect of an Earth other and find some continuity—skin color, for instance—or trace the lines in your palm in continuity with the stem of a leaf or other lines along the ground. Consider your skin membrane that contains yourself apart from this Earth other and yet the common substance that you share. If you prefer a vocal sense of continuity, listen for the sounds of birds or wind or an animal barking or making other sounds, and call back. Extend their song or sound with your own response. You might be surprised by the response you receive if a conversation of sorts springs up between you. Looking for and deliberately invoking these points of continuous contact calls attention to the phenomenal reality that we are always already embedded in relations of creaturely continuity.

CHAPTER TWO

Kinship Experience

Courage—Ecospiritual Senses—Solastalgia

> I have not been nearly as wild as I need to be.[1]

The formal object of study in Christian spirituality is experience.[2] To fully elaborate our kinship experience, we will likely need to spend time in wild places while also recognizing the wild's persistent presence in urban spaces, where many people live in the twenty-first century. To rewild such kinship experience also means deepening our capacity to tolerate what is "wild" about our own identities. Honing our ecospiritual senses enables us to grow in awareness of our kinship relations with creaturely others and what is wild within us and what we need to let go of to let these areas be rehabilitated and relationships flourish, especially when threatened in their integrity. Ecospiritual and ecotherapeutic practices that draw us outdoors and away from the deadening materials and tasks of everyday life change our experience, enabling us to grow into a more intimate relationship with what is natural and wild about our lives, both alone and with others. Rewilding our kinship experience is essential to undoing the damage of our industrialized and domesticated lives, both to our external environments and to our inner ecologies.

We live in a strange time, when our identities and experiences are most often shaped by worlds not physically proximate to ours. Through our routine use of technologies that draw us into digital spaces composed of lives often quite distant from us and our routine consumption of ideas swirling there, we allow ourselves to be taken away from the immediacy of our own bodies and the people and critters with whom we share a life in our neighborhoods. Just as we, longtime members of reading cultures, have routinely inhabited virtual worlds of imagination when engaging in stories and teachings communicated through books, we now routinely inhabit virtual worlds, both visual and aural, that are facilitated through screens of various shapes and sizes. The impact of this new reality on our experience is yet to be fully determined. Today, I walk in a beautiful nearby park and regularly pass people glancing at screens or plugged into words or music that obscure park sounds. While feeling empathy for people for whom these quiet moments immersed in virtual worlds may be therapeutic in their own right, I worry about what deeper therapeutic engagement with the world around them these people are missing. I worry about our capacity to remain present, believing that capacity to remain present fosters our work of appreciation and care.

I write from personal experience here. I want to face with courage the seeming addiction to streaming films and TV series that the recent pandemic exacerbated when many of us were under lockdown. Like others, I suspect that a heightened attachment to online community and online experience formed during this period hasn't yet been replaced by the in-person relationships truly constitutive of our human being. It is remarkable to consider that a phenomenon as recent as some of our technologies can dislocate our minds and senses from our physical worlds. Coming home from school to a regular itinerary of reruns of *Flipper*, *Gentle Ben*, and *The Adventures of Rin Tin Tin* may have helped me understand and empathize with other creature kin and to long for different ways of living with creature kin than was possible to me then, or even now. But I wonder what relationships with the actual critters of my neighborhood these televised relationships substituted for. And how my life would be different had I spent more time learning to be in my body in the outdoors, allowing myself to be formed by the living relationships there. Increasingly, we'll need to reevaluate the benefits associated with digitized versus analog sociality and whether we are content enough with the quality of life shaped for us by them; we'll also need to consider the costs incurred by these benefits, especially those costs borne by the more-than-human.

EXPERIENCE IN THE EREMOCENE

The fifth-century treatise "In Praise of the Desert" drew on the growing body of wisdom associated with the Christian desert dwellers and urged its application within monastic settings, which were no longer primarily found in wild, remote settings but throughout the known world, interacting with and even responsible for the local economies. The desert then became a compelling metaphor for people who would not physically know the desert. Their bodies and senses deprived of the actual, the metaphorical provided an alternative to play with to describe their solitude, whether actual or attempted within. The author of this encomium celebrating the desert, Eucherius of Lyon, explored all the valence associated with biblical deserts to convince his readers of the alignment between their own adopted lifestyles and the precedent set by holy exemplars before them. For instance, because the Israelites wandered in a wilderness and were fed with manna, Eucherius encourages his readers to remember they, too, may have God's visible beneficence when the land cannot provide for them. Similarly, the many references to thirst in the Hebrew Scriptures reflect the Middle Eastern origination of the sacred stories and how readily experience of physical thirst might speak to realities associated with the inner life: thirsting for God, for divine presence, for the sacred, and for that which gives life.

Perhaps the desert can too readily seem a place of unwholesome deprivation for which God's grace appears as a foil. Yet much of the paradox embedded in this metaphor reflects how early monastics recognized God emergent within their solitude, thus coinciding with the desert as a metaphorical environment stripping away all else that seemed to prevent access to, or awareness of, God's ubiquitous presence. Notably, Eucherius writes of the desert as maternal, claiming the desert holds those who find within it a rock, rather than shifting sands, upon which to build their firm dwelling (shades of Matt 7:24–27) "as in their mothers' lap."[3] The desert was the place that protected dwellers therein because of the natural inaccessibility associated with the desert and the existential inaccessibility the monastic chose when withdrawing from worldly occupation. The notion of a "desert of the heart" (*cordis eremus*) speaks to a state of being when the Christian experiences freedom from compulsions associated with "the world." Eucherius is describing temperance mainly in this context and celebrating the abstinent efforts the desert more readily makes possible for the person who dwells there, but the idea of *balance* also aligns with this notion. Rather than regard abstinence or indulgence as ends, the desert Christian used discernment to align their inner and outer ecologies. The pregnant metaphor of the desert suggested possibilities of new identities that could be formed in solitary contemplative engagement with God through the specificity of places where this forming could happen.

We humans are adept at using metaphors to express creatively how we experience life. These metaphors help us evoke realities that seem otherwise unexplainable. We couch our ideas about ourselves in the voluminous ideas and experiences present to us throughout our cultural inheritance of language; this making of connections to fine-tune our communication about ourselves may be one of our gifts as a species. One such metaphor for experience in the twenty-first century is its *impoverishment*. This metaphor reveals our assumption that our experience should be a source of vital nourishment, abundance, and enrichment for us. Our experience is our true wealth. The economic aspect of this particular metaphor accrues paradoxical intensity in a period of consumer capitalism responsible for much of the ecological damage we humans have caused in this world. To identify the diminishment of our contemporary experience with a word ordinarily associated with economics reveals a lot about where our values lie. The connection to something that cannot be commodified means we yet sense the power of experience to operate beyond our typical mechanisms of exchange.

Tied to this metaphor of impoverishment is that of deficit. For instance, *nature-deficit disorder* occurs when we do not have enough experience within the wild world—the kind that typically happens within the framework of unpredictable, spontaneous outdoor play—to become healthy, well-functioning beings.[4] This deficit originates in childhood when children aren't allowed either the freedom or safety to play outdoors and to learn to experience the world as a particular kind of place and part of themselves. The impacts of this deficit, however, can be lifelong, and as a diagnosis, the situation requires treatment, which Richard Louv called vitamin N (N for Nature). In fact, Louv's 2016 book merges ideas associated with economics and health care by using language of vitamin N supporting a "nature-rich" life; his book offers ideas to "enrich" our experiences as family and community.[5] Certainly, this kind of integration is helpful in identifying our true wealth as our body, mind, and soul's integrity and the integral, healthy habitat we require to maintain that wealth.

Another metaphor for experience, likely of particular relevance in the Judeo-Christian traditions, is the metaphor of *exile* or alienation. Built into the story of biblical peoples is an experience of not quite belonging in this world, originating with the story of expulsion from the garden of Eden. Subsequently, removal from land that biblical peoples thought was God-given also remade their identities as peoples wandering and seeking. The pattern embedded in these ancient stories has had a potent effect on modern life as many of us have had to seek jobs, housing, and opportunities in places distant from home and from the families and communities once so essential to our forming. For a lot of people, this removal can constitute an important dimension of healing and growth, so I don't want to oversimplify the perils of exile as a metaphor for contemporary experience; to leave a dysfunctional home or community, as the Israelites did in escaping enslavement in Egypt, may be vital for some. Rather, I do want to express sadness that so many people experience a desire to stay in their homeplaces, where they know they belong and are wanted, yet cannot remain because of systemic forces in which we are all complicit. Here, Indigenous peoples have navigated this reality of dislocation for hundreds of years, and their cultural histories offer a twofold wisdom: we can foster community resilience wherever we're exiled and, as a community, grow intolerant of and transform systems that force us into exile.

Exile as a metaphor, however, reveals how even in places where a person may have grown up, they can become alienated from their physical, natural surroundings by being habituated to household life, to use of a car or personal vehicle, and to employment or activities that keep them indoors. These normalized factors of contemporary human life foster alienation even in a landscape where one has ostensibly been at home one's whole life. These two sides of a metaphor of distancing from the places where we can feel and know our utmost belonging are devastating, causing a severe imbalance in our mental, physical, and spiritual well-being. Exile experience emphasizes dislocation, as if what is real beckons to us from elsewhere, and we endlessly defer appreciation of the real to that elsewhere. This quality of our experience is exacerbated by our virtual technologies, as mentioned earlier, when our bodies are in one place and our minds and attention in another. This bifurcation of our selves is real and may result in evolutionary changes in our species identity over which we have little or no control.

Finally, a critical metaphor for our time is also the *extinction* of experience.[6] This metaphor expresses a heightening awareness of the risks we take in not attending to the changes in our experience previously expressed here as merely impoverishment and exile. While impoverishment and exile suggest, in the first case, diminishment and not erasure and, in the second, that a more abundant life is possible elsewhere, extinction suggests experience is gone. With this metaphor, we express our too-often-suppressed realization that there are certain experiences we no longer can have. As forests vanish due to logging, disease, global warming, and overdevelopment, the experience of wandering in the woods is extinguished. As island nations disappear due to rising tides, the experience of seeing the sun rise or set from particular vantage points is extinguished. As particular animal and plant species go extinct, the experience of particular ranges of biodiversity is extinguished. I focus here on human experience, as it's what we know best, but concomitant to these losses are, of course, the losses to other species. Metaphors of the impoverishment, alienation, and extinction of experience all pertain to other species' experiences of life as well, and we are complicit in this global transformation. Certainly, our domesticated pets have impoverished experiences when we control their fertility and keep them inside a household. I hope that certain other experiences offset some of these deprivations. Though alienation as metaphor is often an existentially felt threat that we can't know whether other species experience, we can certainly see the literal, on-the-ground making of climate refugees among other species. And, finally, the literal extinction of species is making certain experiences no longer possible among other members of our Earth community; as coral reef habitats bleach and perish, for instance, the experience of having these places as a home is extinguished for fish and sea creatures who have housed there.

These metaphors of impoverishment, exile, and extinction of our experience yield a fundamental quality of contemporary life: loneliness. This, too, is not species-specific in that we may heartbreakingly note that the experience extends poignantly to some nonhuman species through their last days. I wonder whether a critical anthropomorphism permits us to attribute loneliness to these critters' experiences. Whether or not they understand what we understand by loneliness, we live in what has been called the Eremocene, or an age of loneliness.[7] This word feels particularly prescient and special to me because *eremos* is the Greek word indicating desert, the place where those early wild Christians withdrew to be more present to themselves, others, and God. The word evokes an erroneous sense that the desert is empty, barren, and lonely, and for some, the desert may be experienced that way. Emptiness and aloneness have characterized desert wilds in the popular imagination for millennia, and so this word is attached to a name for our era. We all live, whether or not we are actual desert dwellers, in a time when we likely experience profound loneliness, which though so normalized that we may hardly be aware of it, features as a quality of life that our ancestors could consider in other contexts. This quality of life exists in paradoxical tension with high population density and the quantity of social media friends and followers that proliferate in our digital worlds.

The loneliness I am describing is not just that of alienation from human communities but is also a *species loneliness*.[8] This term describes a sense of having removed ourselves from vital engagement with members of many other species with whom we coevolved and with whom our recent and our faith ancestors had routine and meaningful relationships. This contemporary cutting off of relationship and kinship means a severe destabilization and change to our human identity, and we are grappling with the resulting symptoms: addiction, depression, distraction, uneasiness, violence, trauma, and more. The loneliness that results in such personal dysfunction also manifests as vulnerability to political manipulation. As Hannah Arendt observed, "What prepares men for totalitarian domination in the non-totalitarian world is the fact that loneliness, once a borderline experience usually suffered in certain marginal social conditions like old age, has become an everyday experience of the ever-growing masses of our century."[9] Our severance from the natural world, though often deemed insignificant, can account for today's existential malaise, manifesting as political, social, cultural, and other forms of dysfunction.

As we consider loneliness as a defining characteristic of our time, we might remember how the second biblical creation account shows that God did not consider it good for humans to be alone. After the first creation story, in which God affirms creation's goodness, we learn that there is one thing in the second story that is *not* good: human loneliness. Unfortunately, the story goes on to show that animal companionship was insufficient to appease human loneliness, and though we can understand the truth of this to some degree, its significance in light of our failure to celebrate interspecies relationships signals support for regarding animal life as less valuable than human life. While we acknowledge the biblical roots of our creature kin being disqualified as a loneliness remedy, let's also acknowledge the wisdom expressed regarding the undesirability of human loneliness and the solution posed, though incomplete: interspecies relationships. What would have happened if our human biblical stories of origin had celebrated and not discounted these relationships? In our time, because we have for centuries and even millennia accepted the insufficiency of other species' companionship, we have neglected to cultivate our relationships and even allowed our attempts to cure our loneliness to amplify destruction to animal habitat and lifeways. These habits have led to a cultural crisis of loneliness that will require our honoring and restoring relationships beyond our species. Our literal lives depend on this restoration.

LANGUAGE TO REWILD OUR ECOSPIRITUAL SENSES

Part of the work of revaluing our interspecies relationships is to realize how much we have in common. Our family resemblances and our sense of the *familiar* even among strange and other species help us recover a sense of our creaturely continuity. This recognition of family resemblance is mediated primarily through our senses but also through our acknowledgment that creature kin navigate their worlds through sensual contact and discernment just as we do. Indeed, the origins of life were all about discernment associated with movement and consumption that could happen only through vestigial sensual acuity. Our ecospiritual senses arise from an awareness that our earthly bodies coevolved with our universe. All our sensory apparatus emerged as responses to a lively world reaching out and offering us ways to make sense of life through our bodies. This is so with our numerous creature kin as well.

In early Christian spiritual tradition, the spiritual senses were posited as the Christian's means for discerning the ways God existed within and communicated through the things of this world. A sacramental theology then emerged that provided a means for understanding the relationship between the divine and materiality. In part, biblical texts were a source of confirming these spiritual senses, as a text like the Song of Songs might elaborate the means by which love is expressed and known through bodily apprehension of the beloved other. This is heightened physical sensation and sacred experience. Other poetic literature of the Bible provides a mixing of senses to highlight how important the senses are in a person's apprehension of the world. Psalm 34 invites the reader to "taste and see" the goodness of God. Knowledge of God's goodness is supposed to be mediated by a sensual dimension of human life (namely, taste). Of course, eating God would become an important element of liturgical life in the Eucharist much later. The psalmist, however, was extolling more everyday feasts, and Song of Songs is full of gustatory delight involving not just the human lover's body but also honey, milk, wine, raisins, apples, figs, walnuts, and pomegranates. Other smells, sights, sounds, and textures are variably present in poetic fragments that celebrate the resonance of life expressed through the human and in other species, animal and vegetal.

The hybrid quality of the sacred text's tending to the literal and metaphorical facilitates our dismantling of a binary between them. For this and other reasons, the Song of Songs and other poetic scriptural texts in the Judeo-Christian tradition have much to remind us about the holistic quality of human life. Subsequent Christian tradition has often made the spiritual senses cerebral, an extension of the mind preoccupied with sacred matters after the body has been disciplined through fasting and sexual abstinence. This cerebral occupation with discerning God's will through engagement with biblical text and through prayer leads ultimately, in the classical mystical itinerary, to divine union. Use of spiritual senses to discern God's will extends throughout the spiritual life, as we learn how to calibrate our own desires with God's and to adjudicate relationships of power and authority among the human community and our sacred texts. Significantly, the spiritual senses affirmed a knowingness in human experience that was thought to transcend the physical senses; intuition and imagination might figure largely in the use of this faculty and allow Christian thinkers to avoid being reductionist about their material lives, positing an elusive sixth sense through which God communicated. Naturally, the elusiveness of this set of senses opens us to wondrous creativity just as much as it does to manipulative misuse.

Rewilding the spiritual senses means to reliteralize them in part and simply celebrate the fact that we are human bodies whose senses can apprehend important information about the world around us and even of the life within us and of which we're constituted. Most of our ability to convey knowledge through our senses is shared with other species. We see and hear in similar manners. Though the content of our seeing or hearing varies, the means by which our bodies' cells and systems come together to respond to that which can be seen, heard, and experienced is similar. This similarity can help us renew kinship relationships. With some species we may share very little, yet that lack helps us widen the definition of our senses. When, for instance, we see that a tree lacks eyes such as we have, we may yet wonder, How does the tree "see"? How does consideration of that means of perception help us revitalize what is meant by "seeing," not as metaphor but as reality refracted through multiple species' experiences? We can apply similar questions with the other senses.

Fundamental to this work of rewilding the spiritual senses is also restoring our relationship with the wild, to actually be in relationship with the wild as we exercise our senses. This essentially means diminishing the role of screens and other human-made products and environments in our experience and engaging with what and who is other, is creature kin, and is thus unpredictable and wild in their relation to us. Permitting our own wildness to emerge through this rekindling of relationship outdoors also revitalizes our capacity to be present with the pain of the world; to be courageous in naming our fears, anger, and grief; and to find ways to watch, listen, smell, taste, and touch for what beckons us into places of renewed responsibility for our creature kin. To do this constitutes an essential re-membering of our constitution as human beings and as the human species. No longer entranced by imagery and stories confined by our own transmissions, we learn to discern other stories and other lifeways that yield wisdom for this time of loss and loneliness. These relationships can, in fact, assuage our loneliness even as they equip us to change our behaviors so that we and others might flourish in community.

The Eremocene as a name for our experience of loneliness draws our twenty-first century lives into resonance with the early Christians rewilding their lives in the deserts of Egypt, Palestine, and Syria. They, too, experienced loneliness even as they were seeking to exchange one set of relationships for another, to replace familial and social obligations with availability for God. I sympathize with their desire, as it aligns with my own frequent hankering to escape all the dysfunction of civilization. However, their loneliness could be a result of their failure to recognize how, as social creatures, we require relationships and how relationships are available to us—even in ostensible solitude—whenever we expand our purview beyond the human.

Not acting on these understandings, many desert dwellers developed what they called *acedia*, which has contours akin to depression but is a general listlessness, apathy, or lack of caring. The fourth-century desert Christian Evagrius described this well, charting the progress of the emotional response to loneliness throughout his day.[10] It might begin as the sun seems to barely move midday but to stay in place, prolonging the experience of acedia. One might then begin to seek distractions in meals or visitors; self-pity at one's loneliness and even hatred toward others who have forgotten one might develop. This is fear of missing out (FOMO) to an exaggerated degree, resulting in a strong desire to abandon one's place, to find meaningful work somewhere else, and to join some other community where one's true value will be recognized. All these variables emerge during a day in which acedia is present. Withstanding temptation to be distracted and to unroot oneself from one's committed place became an important expression of a virtuous, holy life.

Even as we sense resonance with the experience of our ancestors in faith, we are also trying to give new names to experiences these others may not have experienced in quite the way we do now. We've already discussed that nature-deficit disorder is a name ascribed to children being inept at spontaneous outdoor play but expert in video-gaming and other screen-addicted pursuits and the Eremocene is a name given to our era of species loneliness. Scholar-practitioners are attempting to formulate new words that help us understand our contemporary experience in order to evaluate whether this experience might be changed. We intuitively know we are not supposed to be alone, and as this situation grows in reality and intensity, we grieve preemptively. Some have begun talking of *pre-traumatic stress disorder* as being expansively applied to all of us in the throes of recognizing the severity of the losses our worlds are experiencing. Giving expression to these experiences is part of the meaning-making activity that makes us who we are as a species.

Alicia Escott and Heidi Quante formed the Bureau of Linguistical Reality (BLR) as a means to elaborate the new language required of us at this time to mark the concreteness of our experience. This elaboration is a first step toward doing something about our situation. The BLR solicits new words and operates workshops to help people think through and experience how the construction of language helps to identify otherwise bewildering facets of our contemporary life. For instance, one of my favorite neologisms on the BLR's website is *psychic corpus dissonance*. This phrase was created by Escott and Quante in 2014 and expresses

> the conflict between mind and body that occurs when a person experiences unusually warm weather during a time that has historically been considered winter. In this state the body experiences ecstasy to be in unusually warm weather while, simultaneously, the mind experiences worry and concern that weather patterns are deeply amiss, often resulting in a sensation akin to guilt or guilty pleasure.[11]

Further, Escott and Quante offer a usage:

> Basking in the warm winter sun by the beach in San Francisco in January 2014, Heidi and Alicia both experienced psychic corpus

> dissonance as they sat comfortably in their sundresses looking warily at the dry dune scrub flowers blooming unusually too early, both sensing something was amiss with the seasons—an experience they did not have the language to express to one another.[12]

Language may not yet be enough to remedy our experience, but our experience remains wholly private if not communicable with language. Of course, weeping and wailing may be forms of languageless, syntax-less expression, and we may have deep need of that kind of expression and communication, privately and collectively. To elaborate strategies of coping and resilience and move to the facilitating of flourishing called forth from us at this time, however, we need (at least preliminarily) to give words to our experience. What delights me about this application of our courage and creativity is that it is done in community. As Escott and Quante demonstrate, a need to recognize their shared experience resulted in new language. Rather than experience this bewilderment alone and be further entrenched in our age of loneliness, they came together, and their work with the BLR gathers others to construct language to facilitate deeper self-understanding, community resilience, and the lifestyle transformations we all need.

Such has also been Glenn Albrecht's project in giving name to a host of contemporary experiences, primarily of loss. His most famous word was created in 2003 and is *solastalgia*, in which we can hear the echo of *nostalgia*. Albrecht has combined the "sol" of *solace* and desolation with *-algia* (pain) to create this word. Embedded in its middle is *-ast*, evoking *nostos* (home). Though the word originated with Albrecht's own experience of observing how coal mining was impacting a beloved landscape, there is a community aspect here as well, as he sensed that the others who were suffering this landscape transformation would understand the word. The word would call forth and give expression to their shared experience of loss. Similarly, it would function to draw more of us into recognition of our own landscape transformations and how we feel about them. Albrecht writes:

> I define "solastalgia" as the pain or distress caused by the ongoing loss of solace and the sense of desolation connected to the present state of one's home and territory. It is the existential and lived experience of negative environmental change, manifest as an attack on one's sense of place. It is characteristically a chronic condition, tied to the gradual erosion of identity created by the sense of belonging to a particular loved place and a feeling of distress, or psychological desolation, about its unwanted transformation. In direct contrast to the dislocated spatial dimensions of traditionally defined nostalgia, solastalgia is the homesickness you have when you are still located within your home environment.[13]

This loss of identity that is incurred as one loses a vital connection with a formative place is a significant dimension of this experience, one we likely take for granted and feel that we can "get over" as we mature and find other ways to stabilize and articulate our identities.

However, this particular kind of loss is at the root of so many of our cultural and ecological problems right now. It might help us respond to this loss by identifying ways our range of emotions gives expressions to this new reality. In *Earth Emotions*, Albrecht offers a glossary to help us calibrate our emerging experiences and to galvanize action. For example,

- Ecoagnosy: lack of knowledge about, hence ignorance of, past ecological states.
- Terrafurie: extreme anger unleased within those who can clearly see the self-destructive tendencies in the current forms of industrial-technological society and feel they must protest and act to change its direction.
- Topoaversion: the feeling that you do not wish to return to a place that you once loved and enjoyed when you know that it has been irrevocably changed for the worse.[14]

Loss of language accompanies loss of culture, as many Indigenous peoples have experienced. Working to retain, recover, and create aspects of culture, including ceremony and language, may help us all. We may also look to the natural world for models of recuperation, restoration, and resurgence to awaken to the reality of our experience and make deliberate movements toward the experience *we* want to have and to make possible for future generations. It takes courage to examine our experience and realize what may be missing from it, amid the assumptions we have inherited about what success and happiness look like. Material plenitude can mask the isolation and loneliness we feel. Yet in the natural world, of which we're a part, loneliness is hardly even an option except for the human who seeks only their species kind for company. There is plenty of company at hand, anywhere we are. Rather than center our own emotions and experience all the time, we might develop good kin relations with other creatures so that we see in what ways they, too, could experience solastalgia as their homeplaces are devastated by human impact.

A RECIPROCATING ECOSPIRITUALITY

Spirituality is a discipline inviting scholars and practitioners to a closer examination of experience, that of their own and others—typically those who have written books and those with whom we interact today. We should also consider the more-than-human experience. Theories of spiritual formation have emerged from the lives of individual saints and devout people and are applied helpfully at times for others, and many members of faith communities regard their founders' lives as paradigmatic for how they should experience their own lives. Similarly, we might look to animal and plant lives and even the life of water as models for shaping our ecospiritualities. Discernment about how one's life might grow to resemble another revered person's life has led to increasing use of spiritual direction, a venerable and ancient practice in Christianity that can be traced back to the Christian desert tradition. One way these Christians assuaged their loneliness and acedia was to seek out the wise company and guidance of others. Though they mainly directed their attention to human companions, I find it refreshing that they often learned from the desert and from animal denizens in the desert as well.

Though informal in nature, this early form of spiritual accompaniment in the desert led to more formalized training, today undertaken by people in many different faith traditions and within differing programs that emphasize a particular approach to discernment together. Such spiritual direction today allows pairs (a director and a directee) or spiritual companioning groups to come together on a regular basis for the work of spiritual direction, which means each person joins the conversation with an intention to listen for where and how God is showing up in a person's life. While not the same as counseling or other therapies involving conversation, spiritual direction could, in fact, be easily rewilded in the way that contemporary ecopsychologists are rewilding clinical practice as walk-and-talk therapy and one that regards nature ultimately as healer. Indeed, spiritual direction as an experience of mutual accompaniment is already expanding with the creativity of Victoria Loorz, who has initiated an ecospiritual direction program that involves transforming the framework within which such accompaniment occurs. Just as churches of the wild are taking Christian liturgical celebration outdoors, so too can the ecospiritual direction relationship foster shared experiences of the wild.[15] From my own experience of spiritual direction and ecotherapy, I note the following possibilities.

Rewilding spiritual direction is a means of exercising our ecospiritual senses as we bring elements of the natural world into our conversation, too often conducted in a private place where listening and sharing can go deep but is indifferent to the presence of material others. Plants are an easy presence to bring into this place, as can be animal companions. Even a dedicated space with a window can enable those engaged in spiritual direction to look outdoors and register the fact that the natural world is a ubiquitous presence with and a facilitator of the conversation—in a way that directors and directees already understand God, the sacred or divine, a higher power, or some other name for the source and sustainer of life to be always present. Objects shared from the natural world can function as talk pieces when gathered on a table and mulled over for the insights they suggest within a person's situation and relationships. Seasonally changing these objects and their availability within the conversation can spark new understanding.

Another way to rewild spiritual direction would be for director and directee to take their activity of spiritual direction outdoors. This might mean taking a walk together in a nearby park or sitting in a garden space—wherever there is adequate space to be present for the conversation and the listening it entails without distraction. This movement outdoors would allow participants to affirm that attending to the natural world is also a powerful way to discern God's movement in one's life. On a fundamental level, diurnal, seasonal, and other natural cycles are part of our human spiritual lives, and we can participate in the recognition of our embeddedness within the natural world and the vitality of our ecospiritual senses more fully as we learn to discern our own lives' patterns. Noticing especially the ephemeral quality of some aspects of being outdoors, such as changing air temperature or clouds passing in the sky, can be transformatively suggestive in how they resonate with a person's inner life and potential turmoil. Being approached or visited by a wild critter can radically transfigure the tenor of a conversation.[16]

Spiritual direction can also be rewilded, as an emphasis is placed on how God is revealed through the natural world in an explicit way in practices a spiritual director shares with the directee. While in Christian traditions the director might help a person deepen their prayer life or commitment to other traditional practices, a rewilded spiritual direction practice makes room for the invitation to engage practices now aligned with ecotherapeutic practices. Some of the ways that forest therapy guides, for instance, position themselves as facilitators of a forest's healing echo how a spiritual director has always acted as a deep listener to the needs of a person and led their directee to deeper understanding of God's presence. Such practices posit immersion in natural spaces as healing, liberative, and transforming. Certification for some of these therapeutic modalities is emergent and still loosely defined; it should be critiqued when capitulating to consumerist tendencies in human life today, but the need for many of our experiences to be transformed so that they effect a kind of personal and collective reversal of species loneliness is vital.

Mutual accompaniment names this critical work we need to do in coming together to acknowledge our species loneliness and to transform our lifestyles that currently allow us to remain apathetically complicit in normalizing this loneliness. We know, of course, that aloneness is not the same as loneliness and that it is not possible to be alone in this world. Though it may seem counterintuitive to advocate for more time spent alone in the wild, I think we do need to balance our superficial relationships with a great number of people, often played out in virtual spaces, with the interspecies relations available to us when we are in a natural place and without other humans. Walking in some woods or on a beach alone and not being "plugged in" to one's pervasively present electronic device can be an amazingly therapeutic experience. For some, this can feel unsafe. Yet we can work as a community to make it possible for people to be alone in the wild and to be safe. As we learn how essential this is to our overall health and healing, we need to facilitate opportunities for this to happen for each other and to give each other the space to fully benefit from such immersions.

To remember that we are always mutually accompanied by others in the more-than-human world can itself be therapeutic. We tend to think anthropomorphically, attributing to clouds and trees and our companion animals expressions and emotions that we are comfortable with. I've done this in this chapter when attributing what we understand as loneliness to species undergoing extinction. Thinking anthropomorphically when critically aware that we are doing so can be helpful, as it allows us to establish a connection with others who do not bear our shapes but have some semblance of lifeway we recognize as *familiar*—that is, as pertaining to our being, in some sense, *family*.

The first of the 150 biblical psalms elaborates the tree as a being whom the devout reader might emulate, soaking their roots in soil fed by a constantly running stream and yielding leaves and fruit. The "stream of water" for the devout Jew might be the study of the Torah; for Christians, the study of Scripture and other classics in the spiritual tradition can function likewise. Such a poetic image, however, needn't be solely metaphorical. While a metaphor always operates in liminal, nondual space, opting for either literal or metaphorical readings reinforces dualism. We could instead favor both. The reader is invited to take the image metaphorically to speak of their sacred scriptures and to be mindful of the way that the natural world offers lessons about connection: the tree would not exist without the stream, and as we learn more about forest ecosystems, we can see how the stream also would not exist without the tree. We, too, are like the tree and unlike the tree in needing our roots planted deep in places that nourish us.

Psalm 1 issues an invitation to the reader to be as committed to the study of God's law as a tree is inevitably rooted to a spot next to a water source, drawing sustenance through roots sunk into deep terrain. This image reveals the psalmist's understanding of how human and trees are kin. The tree models a way of fidelity and even a naturalness about the source of the tree's sustenance that humans might also experience. So many human encounters with the divine occur at trees or within sacred groves. Historically, the tree has functioned as an important site of wisdom seeking, judgment, discernment, and discernment. Despite the resemblances with humans (i.e., the words *trunk* and *limbs* naming allied parts), the tree is fundamentally other and allows us to glimpse something of the nonhuman God and discern God's will. In the case of the psalm, we hear about the natural life cycle of the tree: the drawing up of needed water; the bearing of fruit, including blossoming and fertilization and the insects and birds inhabiting the tree's branches; and the vitality of the tree's leaves, harbinger of the visionary experience of John of the Revelation and the healing trees of new Jerusalem (Rev 22:2).

It is curious to me that some other wisdom traditions consider physical emulation of creature kin as a means of practice, that embodying the natural other is a means of one's fulfillment. Thus, the many postures associated with Tai Chi enable a person to realize that the fluidity of their movements is akin to water's movement or to a crane's flying. Many yoga postures are named after aspects of our creature kin and the ways our own human bodies reassemble themselves around these forms in ways that are natural to us, though often unpracticed in everyday life and encounters. Even the Buddhist seated in meditation emulates a lotus flower in the stilling of body, folding of legs, and straightening of spine. This becoming the animal or vegetal or even mountain other is a means of living the practice of ourselves in our own bodies, paradoxically, through the other. Christianity seems to have less of this emphasis in our practices, though our literature of Christian spirituality habitually uses imagery drawn from creation to speak of our own human identity and capacity.

Perhaps we Christian practitioners think of likeness to other lifeforms as simply that—likeness—to be assented to intellectually and not necessarily embodied. Thus, we note the resemblance to a tree's lifeway that Psalm 1 asks us to model our study on and then go our own way, rarely consciously thinking of ourselves as tree-like or regarding the source(s) of our being as vitally compelling as the streams of water. We jump too hastily to metaphorical thinking without considering the value of taking what is suggested literally. We also fail to engage with other works of Christian spiritual literature on their own terms, which includes following practices that would require us to embody the truths of our kinship with other creatures and thus treating them with more respect than we might otherwise.

Such creature kin become our spiritual teachers, spiritual directors, gurus, and mentors with whom or to whom we disciple ourselves. But I sense they invite us to a radically different kind of relationship beyond the master–disciple relationships operative throughout wisdom traditions worldwide. Rather than this hierarchical relationship, the biodiversity and cooperation of the more-than-human world remind us that each has a place of simultaneously embodying learner and teacher for and with each other. This is mutual accompaniment and helps us to elaborate what we might call a phytomorphic, zoomorphic, or aquamorphic ecospirituality and ecospiritual practice.

Phytomorphic ecospirituality refers to the resemblance we bear with all beings vegetal. Psalm 1 expresses a phytomorphic ecospirituality in expressing the resemblance between tree and human life in centering well-being as proximity to a nourishing source. Likewise, my favorite saying of the Christian desert tradition expresses a phytomorphic sensibility when it advises, "In the same way that no plant whatsoever grows up on a well-trodden highway, not even if you sow seed, because the surface is trodden down, so it is with us. Withdraw from all business into *hesychia* (or quietness) and you will see things growing that you did not know were in you, for you were walking on them."[17] In this saying, *hesychia* is proposed as an antidote to acedia in that being still, resisting the pull to distractions, means the potential for dispersing tensions unhelpful for maturity in the spiritual life and for the revealing of one's integral authenticity. We use so many casual phrases that evince a recognition that plant life models something really important for us about stability, in particular, because of the rootedness of plant life. In recent years, recognition of the rhizomatic quality of certain plants to distribute roots from various places rather than from one place, such as a tree does, has helped the human community think about different operations and ways of being human community that foster resilience. This quality evokes for me the principle of diversification and invites me to consider, as a spirituality scholar-practitioner, the ways my own resilience as a human being is fostered by feeling rooted at multiple places. Rather than conceive this variable rootedness as a liability, a kind of weakening of firm commitment to one enterprise, this rhizomatic quality of Christian spirituality as a discipline might mean that a scholar has multiple points of entry into the field, multiple places where their interests are fed to nourish their spiritual well-being. For me, the Christian desert tradition, ecospirituality, and the arts all function as various roots with things in common but separate for various reasons.

Other approaches to counterbalancing our predominantly anthropocentric and anthropomorphizing tendencies would be to consider other ways that life is modeled in various other nonhuman forms. The zoomorphic refers to animal form and the aquamorphic to water form. Of course, we *are* animals, so it may be odd to consider a word that speaks to other animal life as a model for our own, but one option for the zoomorphic is to express how other animals' life-forms are expressed in the human. Notably, we often use language of the animal to degrade our human experience or identities, and this tendency reveals our distortion of values and imposition of our own detested qualities on animals that we might justify oppressing for this identification. Many feminists, in particular, have pointed out the connections between exploitation of women and animals and the various names that draw from animal identities to demean women. Reconfiguring our values means we wouldn't consider it an insult to be identified with animal life, recognizing the natural correspondence with our animal being and even inviting deeper identification through it.

Water figures as an important constitutive element of our human life, even as we see how water models something important about the world outside our bodies. In being fluid and generating soft power, we see models of our own transcorporeality and how persistence over time can yield significant change. In the Christian desert tradition, of course, water was important as a cherished, rare part of nature that could figure along the lines of biblical expressions when the soul, says the psalmist, thirsted for God (Ps 42). In the Middle Eastern and African contexts of early Christianity, thirst was an experience that taught people through their bodies how to regard God. One desert Christian taught: "The nature of water is soft, that of rock is hard, but a [dripping] vessel hung above a rock pierces the rock, little by little. Likewise, the word of God is soft, but our heart is hard. When one often hears the Word of God, [their] heart is opened to fear God."[18] Though this saying uses water to indicate elements of Christian spiritual practice that provide sustenance and refreshment and that subtly transform a person over time, I hear an invitation to expose our lives to the natural elements, water included, to be transformed. In our bodies, our transcorporeality is effected as we slowly erode and shed the systemic imprints of traumatic experiences, loneliness being among them.

As Christian spirituality scholars, we invite creativity as we use more names to clarify how we understand these other creature kin to operate as our community partners in scholarship, in the development of deeper self-understanding, in mutual accompaniment in our spiritual and ecospiritual practice, and more. Similarly, we call on our reservoirs of courage in using our creativity to name new experiences of the Eremocene as Alicia Escott, Heidi Quante, and Glenn Albrecht have done. Facing our losses and developing a willingness to be vulnerable in sharing what most angers and grieves us, though painful processes, will not only heal fragmented human communities but also create the means by which regeneration and flourishing throughout creation can begin. And while this chapter has focused mostly on experiences that we might label negative, there are also lots of other, more positive experiences to both name and create space for. Our fixation on the negative is natural, and we need it. It is not to shame but to normalize feelings that are uncomfortable. On the other side of that fixation and normalization, we can also acknowledge that all creatures, human and more-than-human, have capacity for joy and delight. As we create the opportunities for this kind of experience to grow again, we also need new words to name these experiences and practices to draw our awareness to these experiences.

Starting here with the body and our own experiences, we can tend to what is vital in our calling to care for particular creature kin and to foster ways of life that do the least harm to those creature kin. This is not self-indulgent work, as it may appear. I realize that in a time of grievous loss and harm, to let ourselves be at play in the wild to hone our ecospiritual senses may seem silly. I sense it is a vital means, however, of satisfying our deepest longings, particularly of species loneliness. While I'm not advocating that a relationship with the wild substitute for human relationships, I am advocating for a restoration of where we look for company and for a removal of our attention from the things that keep us from the company available to us in the wild—even outside our front door and into the streets of our neighborhoods. Beginning to merely notice the wild neighbors around and in our houses, in our streets and cities, is an important transformation of our experience. I sense the loneliness of the natural world is calling to us humans to restore some sense of community more broadly. It may be arrogance to think we're somehow missing from the larger Earth community but simultaneously having such an outsized and devastating impact through our inattention. There is important work to do to restore our creaturely kin relations with others through a critical recognition of our experience today and our ability to change that experience.

If you were a cedar
    you would be waiting for rain to fall
or fall harder, relaxing your ten thousand needles.

If you were a handful of moss
    you would be waiting for the light so you could
climb further up this rich, fallen log.

If you were a blue mussel
    you would be waiting for the tide to rise
to open your lips, to sip.

What a world this is.
    Close your eyes and inhale. Eat a little
of this air. Let it fill your belly. Let the taste of this place
    always rest on your tongue.[19]

ECOSPIRITUAL KINSHIP PRACTICE: RADICAL RECIPROCITY

An important dimension of forest bathing or therapy is awakening our senses. Practices facilitated by a guide often will invite our slowing down and attending to our sensual apprehension of the forest, for instance, and can also be experienced in the mountains, deserts, prairies, coasts, and other places of our outdoor dwelling. This kinship practice asks us to courageously face the decentering of our experience as subjects and to encounter our creaturely continuity with the web of life by playing between the subject–object dualism that is such a part of our everyday experience. This play helps restore a sense of creation's power to move and to heal us; it also restores a sense of creation's agency quite beyond our own controls.

Outdoors, begin by engaging your sense of sight. What do you see? Whom do you see? What variances of shadow and light, of textures, can you perceive? As you settle into this enhanced awareness of your surroundings, consider the following as well: How are you perceived? What do others see when they see, or sense, you? Take a few moments to consider and to really feel this oscillation between your subjectivity as seer and your being seen by another. You are both seer and seen. Then, shift to your sense of hearing. What do you hear? Whom do you hear? Can you distinguish between sounds near to and far from you, between natural and mechanized sounds? Again, consider and feel yourself as both the hearer and the heard. What sounds are others in your vicinity aware of your making? Can your breath be perceived, your heartbeat, your steps on crackling twigs? You are both hearer and heard.

Follow through with other senses. With your sense of smell, breathe deeply of your surroundings. What can you perceive through your olfactory nerves, and what fragrances is your own body giving off so subtly that you may not even notice but with which the creatures around you are more attuned? You are both smeller and smelled. If you feel up to an unusual contact with the outdoors, when you shift to your sense of taste, stick your tongue out and taste the air. Breathe in through your open mouth and consider the freshness of the air and its taste. Can you discern its nuance? In terms of being tasted, you may be "lucky," if in a buggy place or time of year, to discern this quality of your experience readily; otherwise, it could be difficult. Turn your attention to your body's surface and within to consider how these miniscule organisms feast on your dead skin cells and other tissues, helping you chafe off the old and regenerate with room for the new. You are both taster and tasted.

Finally, shift to the sense of touch. Your body is in constant contact with the ground under your feet, or whatever part of your body communicates with the ground, and in constant contact with the air that surrounds you. You are being touched even when you stand alone. Consider the oscillation under your feet as a means of evoking your touching and being touched, in a way that is both within your control and outside of your control. Ponder the safety this kind of touch offers you if touch is not typically a safe expression of being. If near to a tree or bush, reach your hand to the bark or stem and consider the back and forth of touching and being touched. Ponder the vegetal being's consent in your mutual touch and be careful about the pressure you share with this other being. This kinship practice is not to focus on your own ability to damage but rather to restore your understanding of agency in all beings around you. This is difficult to sense in the play of touch when it seems you are the only one making a decision to lean into the contact. For this reason, play with variations on how touch could be expressed. Put yourself in the way of being touched by another so that choice may be expressed by a breeze moving into you, for instance, or in other ways that render you a bit more passive. Be open to the reciprocity suggested by kinship play relationships. You are both toucher and touched.

CHAPTER THREE

Kinship Practice

Curiosity—Discernment—Terraspiritual Inquiry

> Be your naturalness, then commit to the lively disciplines such naturalness is calling forth in you.[1]

Spiritual practice is a component of our lives constitutive of meaning-making. Sometimes such practice allows us to express lament and celebration as well. The rewilding of spiritual practices allows these habits of the heart to draw us into deeper communion with God. Rewilding also challenges and changes an orientation within the field of Christian spirituality to consider spiritual formation as fundamentally a theological-anthropological endeavor, something humans do primarily in relation to God. Rewilding spiritual practice means addressing ecological realities otherwise obstructed by our commitment to normative practice. Thomas Berry wrote that our approach to our work has historically gone through various stages or "mediations," involving a focus on God (the theological), on our human community (the anthropological), and now on our Earth community (the ecological).[2] While acknowledging the field's reliance on human and divine exemplars for modeling behaviors that are commodified as spiritual practices, we can also nuance or even undermine the predominance of this modeling. For instance, we can describe our formation as wild creatures in a wild world as more fundamentally real and indeed *spiritual* than what our narrow focus on saintly humans has permitted us to see and experience. What I mean by this is suggested by Thomas Merton when he muses that a tree gives glory to God by expressing the tree's treeness[3] and by the mythologist Martin Shaw when he refers to our own naturalness giving rise to "lively" disciplines (see this chapter's epigraph).

Practice is among my favorite aspects of Christian spirituality, as my own identity has been shaped by a history of immensely satisfying and pleasurable hours practicing music at a piano. I can appreciate the idea that change happens incrementally through dogged devotion to developing skills and yet surprisingly when all at once we find ourselves in the "flow." Sometimes through the dullest commitment to routine, something suddenly shifts and we're able to do something we didn't think we could do before. This repetition is about creating capacity for spontaneity and a certain kind of fluidity to our everyday actions that can be lacking if we don't cultivate some kind of disciplined behaviors. We might also think of sports as offering a particular activity through which to view spiritual practice. Both musical and athletic practice provide opportunities to anticipate the demands of performance on the stage, court, track, or field, either alone or with others. Both music and sports are human activities that explicitly draw out enhancement over time. However, *most* of what we do habitually and with intention changes us over time, with or without our making quite so big a deal about it.

That music and sports ready a musician or athlete for performance allows us to think about what other intentional practices ready us for. If a major component of our practice is simply heightening our awareness of and experiencing the presence of God, the divine, or sacred, then certainly the experience warrants the time and energy to pursue and repeat it. In that sense, there is no future performance to be aimed at developing capacity; rather, the practice opens up realization of this capacity any time and any place the practice begins. On the other hand, many spiritual practices have side benefits, such as the development of virtuous dimensions of our personality: qualities like patience, generosity, and compassion. And when the time comes, spontaneously, unpredictably, even wildly, these capacities enable us to meet what is demanded of us a bit more effortlessly and skillfully than if we had not prepared through spiritual practice. We become capable of responses informed by patience, generosity, and compassion just as a musician might render a Chopin nocturne movingly or a basketball player might sink the ball from half-court with an elegant swish.

The "wild virtue of curiosity"[4] is one dimension of this work of spiritual practice and, like practice itself, correlates well with music and sports. For as we grow more curious about the other—whether scales, keys, and harmonies or the way our teammates move, prompting collaborative action toward some end—the more we understand about ourselves, others, and our capacities. In spiritual practice, we cultivate curiosity as we engage what is hard about staying put, for instance, in prayer and meditation when our preoccupying thoughts seem to assail us. Certainly, our ancestors in the faith experienced the same difficulties! We can also cultivate curiosity about why a particular practice draws us in effortlessly and feels really good some days but becomes excruciatingly hard other days. In this way, we experience the dynamism of our own identities and learn to withhold judgment from ourselves, thus practicing to withhold judgment of others, as we learn more about why we can, or cannot, engage certain practices meaningfully at any given time. In ecospiritual practice, we extend this curiosity to begin to discern how our preferences impinge on the lives of others. When we see there is a negative impact, can we have the courage to change or to consider carefully the costs involved in remaining committed to the practice?

SUSPENDING SPIRITUAL PRACTICE?

In *Ritual at World's End*, theologian, liturgist, and artist Cláudio Carvalhaes grapples with liturgy as a continuance of business as usual and echoes Jewish theologian and ethicist Marc Ellis's claim that there must be no liturgy until there is justice. Carvalhaes documents an instance of halted liturgy where the Eucharistic table was prepared and the presider said the assembled were not ready to receive, because injustice continued to shape the context in which the Eucharist had been prepared and the context in which its participants came together.[5] As Carvalhaes describes this intervention, he includes the pushback from some participants, who protested that it was not up to the presider to decide whether people could participate in the ritual. Recently in some Roman Catholic contexts in the United States, for example, we have seen how the Eucharist has been instrumentalized to make a point about excluding from participation those whose values do not align with those in power.

I sympathize with the presider's intention to mark the dissonance between the ritual engagement and the everyday context in which it was embedded. While injustice was shaping the relationships between people assembled for liturgy, how indeed could they set that aside to participate? Or shouldn't the liturgy be an occasion for addressing injustice? This issue may not be resolved, but it certainly draws attention to what we expect liturgy to do and what we expect of ourselves and others as we prepare to engage in liturgy. I read this episode in Carvalhaes's book with interest and could not help reflecting on my own disciplinary setting of Christian spirituality. What if we were to regard the paraphernalia of our spiritual practice—our meditation cushions and apps, prayer shawls and phylacteries, devotionals and mantras, singing bowls and gongs, yoga clothes and mats—as requiring us to let them sit idly by, unused until there is justice? What would this mean for us, for our scholarship and teaching and ministries of care? We must call for a suspension of our work if it does not demand of us an expression of our integrity in the form of caring compassionately for others and the earth. Doing the work, then, becomes our essential spiritual practice. We don't wait until our prayer or meditation softens our hearts or dismantles our colonized imaginations, but we act from a place where we already hear the call to liberation and the work to *liberate* in a quite material and everyday manner.

A halt to liturgy happened globally as the COVID-19 pandemic required policymakers to legislate whether it was permitted for a faith community's members to assemble for liturgy. Many communities of faith had to literally remake their liturgies online to facilitate participation. I remember being the last to preach at my church before our COVID shutdown. On March 15, 2020, attendance at Mass was considerably abbreviated as news was forecasting continued spikes in infection and hospitalization in Oregon. I remember the priest of our parish saying I didn't need to preach that day; he would fill in at the last minute, but I was ready. I was ready to lead the few assembled in a guided meditation on what we were going through, on attending to the fullness of the experience. I did that and then spent months online observing Mass more than participating. I grew haphazard, as I imagine others may have, with allowing myself a second cup of coffee as I "watched" Mass, even knitting through Mass on many occasions. I'm not saying handwork doesn't facilitate Mass participation, but in my case, it was a clear alternative to being as engaged as I was used to being when actually present in the sanctuary with others.

I wonder if such a halt to liturgy facilitated a deepening of spiritual practice. When ritual participation in our communities was impossible, did our spiritual practices proliferate? Did we flounder, realizing how much we relied on the container that a faith community provided for regular, meaningful soul-nourishment and not knowing exactly what to do when left to our own devices? It may be too early to tell what the positive and negative impacts on our spiritual lives during COVID have been. Many of us may have found ourselves doing both: becoming more creative *and* feeling at a loss. For some of us, COVID may have initiated us into a personalized, self-care regimen that was and may remain important to us but does not attend to the grievances at large in the world, both social and ecological. We grew to know a lot about essential workers and their vulnerabilities during this recent period of pandemic. It's worth reflecting on whether that knowledge simply accompanied our adoption of personal self-care practices to manage anxiety during our times of isolation as *in*essential workers or whether it helped us put more energy behind working for justice. A similar halt to spiritual practice may be called for at this time as we change our understanding of spiritual practice. We need to be people whose spiritual practices emerge from the work of liberation we do with and for one another and with and for the Earth community. I envision a radical revisioning of spiritual practice, a rekindling of its significance within lives that are attentive to what we and others—human and more-than-human—need. Spiritual practice becomes *eco*spiritual practice. Spiritual practice rewilded. Spiritual practice that cultivates our radical kinship.

Part of this revisioning of ecospiritual practice is merely becoming transparent about our life's commitments without judgment and without regarding any such commitments as the final form our lives might take. Our acceptance of our life's dynamism could also help us live into the flow of adopting some practices at some time while abandoning them at others; meanwhile, we grow the capacity to discern the suitable time for the practice to emerge and disappear. Our transparency about these commitments—and even experimentations—would then take the form of accompanying some of our other work: our scholarship, our mentoring, and so on. We would name the commitments that undergird our work, helping us to have lively pictures of what particular practices look like when embodied in the lifeway of a friend or colleague. I know when I listen to a wise person's thinking, I wonder about their commitments. What ways are they honoring kinship relations in their dietary choices, family planning choices, transportation choices, leisure time choices, and various consumer choices? It may be a bit nosy of me to want the answers to these questions, but the aligning of our theory and practice in light of our climate emergency, in whatever stage where we live, requires that we become more open to these kinds of conversations and more experimental, too, in what we try.

GREEN ASCETICISM AND IDIORRHYTHMIA

The rewilding of practice also requires that we consider the typical mystical itinerary and the ways practice has traditionally interlocked with aspects of practices involving the body, mind, and spirit. For instance, asceticism has typically been associated with preliminary practices that get the body "in shape" for spiritual growth, tending to such issues as one's legitimate though varyingly strong attachment to food, sleep, and other bodily needs. Having dealt with these, theologians considered a person ready to engage their intellect and cognitive faculties to read, meditate on, and pray with texts or other things designed to engage and challenge their thinking skills and beliefs about themselves and others and to form their insight. Finally, the experience of union with the divine happens through fine-tuned awareness of the ubiquity of God's presence always, everywhere, though not always experienced as such. Significantly, a preliminary to this final stage of experience of divine union is a dark night when our intellect's faculties fail us and all our previous understandings about ourselves and God are dismantled. The mystic's appreciation of this final stage often emerges through poetry, song, imagery, and evocation—the truly divine is thought to remain so radically beyond our human comprehension and yet so paradoxically close to our human being as to constitute the ground of our being. Though many have considered this "ground" metaphysically, it's useful to consider its linguistic connection with Earth. This aspect of our being draws God into all that makes it possible for us to sustain life: the air we breathe, the food we eat, the water we drink, and other aspects of our physical lives that require materiality to subsist. The typical itinerary of the mystical, or spiritual, life determines much of where we put our energies as we begin spiritual practices or enhance those we have already adopted.

The Benedictine scholar Columba Stewart has expertly interpreted the agricultural metaphor embedded in ascetic practice in the literature of the Christian desert tradition. In his important article "The Greening of Asceticism," he recontextualizes asceticism for our time, stating its importance as a dimension of practice, particularly for Christians, whose worldview is deeply shaped by an incarnational theology. He claims, and it is noteworthy he was making this claim in the early 1990s: "The recovery of a truly incarnational understanding of asceticism from false spiritualization is critical for Christians who want to engage with the deepest crisis of our time, the systematic ravaging of our primary contemplative medium, the earth on which we live."[6] This means reverence for the vital connection we have with all that sustains life and a willingness to restrain ourselves from discounting the sacredness of this vital connection and instead directing our attention to immaterial things.

Why do we tend to redirect our attention in this way, to the intangible? My sense is that power relations are a part of the answer. It has been easy for some to convince us that they can control this intangible part of us when we have so little facility in seeing or otherwise discerning effects upon "it." The damage that we wield in the world when preferring to attend to the immaterial and the transcendent, however, is so tragic as to evoke our consciousness to exercise respectful restraint in using material sources. And we must learn to value these material aspects of our lives so much that we honor them with the words we usually reserve for the soul: *holiness, the sacred, divinity*, and so on.

Asceticism isn't perhaps the most attractive word to pair with spiritual practice as it can feel to many as *too* disciplinary, rigid, and sacrificial. On the other hand, Fr. Columba's description of recovering a truly incarnational understanding of asceticism means appreciating the importance of our bodies and the body of the earth. He writes,

> The ascetical starting point is the discovery of balance within our own lives as we learn what our bodies need for food, drink, sleep and what they can or cannot tolerate in the way of excess or deprivation . . . The way to do this is to seek a regular diet and other patterns of consumption that abuse neither the body nor conscience nor earth.[7]

Knowing what our bodies need and holding that in balance with what Earth and our Earth community members need to thrive is the work of asceticism. Both activities require discernment and a willingness to acknowledge and change the consumption patterns many of us have inherited and may even feel entitled to. In this way, balance might indeed require the sacrifice of things to which we have become accustomed yet create an imbalance in taking them from others whose legitimate need outweighs our own constructed need. Pope Francis writes impressively of "drastic" changes we need to be willing to make, for instance, in regard to energy use in his recent apostolic exhortation, *Laudate Deum*, a kind of supplement to his 2015 *Laudato Si'*.[8] I love how Episcopal priest David Keller writes of early Christian asceticism as the development of easily satisfied needs,[9] which might help us rehabilitate this aspect of our spiritual practice as we learn that some things available to us to meet our needs are free. These include being outdoors, being in relationship, celebrating our creature kinship, and even participating in many of the arts of movement and making that spring from our species identity. Just as asceticism was once characterized as *red* when it might lead to a martyr's death or *white* when it was bloodless and conducted as fasting or vigil kept within the privacy of one's household, monastic dwelling, church, or village, so today a *green* or rewilded asceticism aligns the body's needs with the Earth body's needs.

Martyrdom, however, as a concrete expression of the ascetic life has been transfigured in the current moment as activists who are people of faith literally put their lives on the line to protest the damaging of and to protect our biological home. This new emergence of faith-inspired activism takes the name ecomartyrdom,[10] and it helpfully dismantles the distinction between social and climate justice as ecomartyrs witness the inextricable connections between both. An ecoasceticism, or green asceticism, suggests a similar protesting of actions complicit in environmental and social destruction and a withdrawal from these actions while recognizing the limited means we each have to do this. Such ecoasceticism may not lead to physical death, but it will lead to the death of certain normative structures within which we live, especially if enough people engage in ecoascetic behaviors. Death to capitalism. Death to extractivism. Death to patriarchy. Death to white supremacy. The discipline involved in refraining from activities complicit in these structures does not develop automatically; indeed, some of us may not even notice that we could opt to say "no" to these structures. Those benefiting from the injustice embedded within these structures require us to remain being distracted, being overwhelmed, and feeling powerless.

The examples of ecoascetics and ecomartyrs instead remind us of the cost involved in our not only resisting these structures but also maintaining them. The short-term payoff may allow us to feel comfortable, but thinking of our and our kin's futures should give us pause. While grim prognostications of our inability to change anything and our likely species demise are often enough to paralyze us from acting, learning and having the discipline to live within legitimate limits that emerge from celebrating our individual gifts and capacities can render this time more joyful than not, even if challenging. The same challenge that a musician and athlete can feel in training their attention to adapt skills with the instruments of their craft can be ours as we learn to live (again) from the real creatureliness we are.

Stewart writes of the agricultural metaphor of working the earth of one's heart: "The contemplative ascetic who works the earth of the heart can learn to work the earth of the planet with open eyes and ears. This challenge requires the use of every human faculty and kind of knowledge as we learn the workings of the cosmos and understand our relationship to it."[11] Gaining new and renewed awareness of our kinship relationships with all that is, we grow a desire for living in better balance with all that is. Doing so moves us into greater appreciation for diversity, as not everybody's needs will be the same or satisfied in the same way, across and within species. Similarly, our diversely adopted ecospiritual practices emerge from our unique capacities. Though all humans share a need to reconnect and experience that reconnection with the more-than-human world, how we do so may vary.

The desert Christians had a word for this diversity of life expression and how a spiritual practice might be cultivated to respond to individual needs and capacities, riding, of course, the razor edge between self-indulgence and self-neglect, excess, and deprivation.

Idiorrhythmia, an individual's own rhythm of life, described how a person's spiritual practice meant walking to the beat of their own drum. Just as the word sounds, the individual rhythm of one's life was respected with no standardizing of practice yet imposed on desert dwellers, though (not surprisingly) such standardization was slowly developing. A desert story tells that

> Abba Lot went to see Abba Joseph and said to him, "Abba, as far as I can I say my little office, I fast a little, I pray and meditate, I live in peace and as far as I can, I purify my thoughts. What else can I do?" Then the old man stood up and stretched his hands towards heaven. His fingers became like ten lamps of fire and he said to him, "If you will, you can become all flame."[12]

This brief tale contains a small catalogue of desert spiritual practices important to many of the protomonks—or as I've argued elsewhere, the Christians—of the Egyptian desert.[13] Though some stories that sensationalized the more extreme feats of these Christians were preserved, in this story we hear the influence of moderation on the desert dweller: the little office, or regular prayer practice with the psalms, a little fasting. Nothing extreme here but an expression of what any devout Christian of this period likely valued in terms of their own virtuous formation, growing capacity for dwelling with God and others and moderating their own needs while being responsive to those of others. Not good enough, the elder Joseph seems to intimate. Better to become "all flame," metaphorically bespeaking the Christian's union with the divine. This story contains in miniature the mystical itinerary and requires a possible corrective, inviting our semblance to fire to remind us how we consume and are consumed. Bodily and intellectual practices develop the capacity of the will to surrender to merging with the flame of divine love. Practices engaging the body and mind aren't to be left behind when one begins to experience the flame of divine love; rather, they are continually and cyclically engaged again and again in a holistic engagement of one's entire being through practice, as a way of more fully inhabiting one's naturalness. Indeed, we become what we already are, realizing this being in an ever more fully realized manner.

Coming together at times (e.g., the weekend) to celebrate parts of the Mass, the desert Christians might have cultivated competition among themselves for whose way of life best exhibited self-sacrifice and devotion to God, thus to be witnessed and marveled at. But they also seemed to espouse respect for each other's various ways of becoming "perfect." I go back and forth in my respect for the tradition in its use of competition and practical idiorrhythmia. A healthy dose of competition among those wanting to adopt behaviors that are ecologically sound might be fruitful in moving the masses in a certain direction. Yet a competitive mindset, especially when tied to notions of scarcity and winner takes all, has been at the root of the problems leading to our current crises. Loosening ourselves from competition would go a long way toward making possible the important conversations we need to have about our ecospiritual practice.

Rewilding asceticism means attending to the individual character of our personal and communal gifts and vulnerabilities. Self-mortification (the dying of the self) was an aspect of traditional ascetic practice, and the more extreme the lengths one went to prove one's mettle as an ascetic, the better. Today, however, our rewilded discipline means living within our species limits, as defined by relationships with other members of our Earth community. We then might develop a kind of Earth rhythm, or ecorrhythmia, a rewilded ascetic practice that requires we adjust our bodily needs so that what we use doesn't negatively impact others. We neither harm nor indulge ourselves by the choices we make to sustain our physical, mental, and spiritual lives. And we grow in awareness about the ethical dimensions of our daily choices; indeed, these choices constitute our ecospiritual practice. A wild ethics, then, should inform what we do and how we do it. This requires discernment, a vital dimension to ecospiritual life. Before that discernment is even possible, though, we may also affirm that a naturalness of our doing arises from our being. The radical acceptance of our being is the basis from which our ecospiritual practices emerge.

Our identities, too, change with this kind of work. The Christian desert tradition has fascinating stories of bodily change through practice. Though the imagery may suggest metaphor, I sense a radical creaturely continuity emergent in the very flesh of these desert dwellers, whose holy humanity came to be figured in the animal. For instance, Bane was a man who lived in the Egyptian desert and stood and walked for much of his life, distributing alms that he had received from officials of the district (who greatly feared him for his holiness) to the poor. For some reason, Bane's exemplarity consists of his standing ascesis and his regimen to not eat while he was involved in distributing money. The story about him tells that he stood for so much of his life that the bones of his feet came to resemble the hooves of deer.[14] Other desert Christians were known as grazers for their preference in living the freedom of the antelopes or buffaloes. One story tells how a desert Christian identified so much with the grazing buffalo that he let himself be captured in a trap and would not use his human capacity to escape, instead acting as the buffalo would have if the buffalo had been entrapped. When the trappers came to release him, he said nothing but left the men and returned to running with the buffaloes.[15]

Black feminist Alexis Pauline Gumbs writes convincingly of the transcorporeal nature of practice in *Undrowned* when she describes in a chapter dedicated to practice how dolphins developed dorsal fins—what we understand now as a constitutive dimension of their identity. Gumbs writes that dolphins "evolved the dense tissue that became dorsal fins *because they needed to* in order to live in the wild movement of the ocean. In other words, dolphins evolved dorsal fins from practice across generations. By accepting that the ocean would always move, and becoming accordingly. An embodied emphasis towards balance."[16] Learning how dolphins use their dorsal fins to stabilize themselves in water, Gumbs clues us into something about our own experience too. What *is* it that we do, habitually, to help stabilize our experience in the world? What did we do during the tumultuous period of COVID-19? During the ongoing tumultuous periods of racial reckoning, Indigenous resurgence, unsettling of our haunted histories, and challenges to our capitalist economic structures? How are these practices that grow out from our body's needs given the particular contexts in which we move?

We help each other pattern what works well even as we honor our species diversity and our ecorrhythmia in adopting particular rhythms of life that work with and for our individually abled bodies. I like Gumbs's working with the dorsal fin a bit better than the aforementioned agricultural image of working the soil of one's heart because of its emergence from the body rather than being a tool that accompanies the body. Both images, however, help us understand and appreciate our profound resonance with the more-than-human and to adopt practices that restore our species balance in relation to other members of the Earth community. Such practices are both constitutive of the beings we are and an ethical response to the balancing of personal and collective needs. Being curious about how our actions positively or negatively impact others invites us to the rigorous work of transforming our spiritual practice so that it no longer just cultivates our inner ecologies in a particular, desired way. Instead, it also cultivates the connections between ourselves and others that is so vital a dimension of our rewilded humanity.

REWILDING DISCERNMENT AND ECOSPIRITUAL EXERCISES

Rewilded discernment, similarly, requires that we slow down and pay attention. Within the Christian desert tradition, discernment is the process for which there are the most teachings and anecdotes in the sayings collections. The fundamental importance of this virtuous activity draws from its enabling a person to subsequently make other decisions and respond compassionately to self and other as need arises. If we don't take the time to develop awareness, we won't be able to respond skillfully as need arises, emergent as the dynamic processes we ourselves are as we adjust to a more strenuous, even sacrificial, activity when necessary and to a more abundant, celebratory activity at others. Centuries after the desert Christians, Ignatius of Loyola developed tools for practicing discernment, which included considering at midday or day's end when we noticed God's presence and when we didn't, when we felt *consolation* and when we felt *desolation*. Importantly, within Ignatian spiritual traditions, the emotions are not aspects of our humanity to deny or ignore. Rather, they communicate meaningfully about what's right for us and for others with whom we live. Rewilding discernment invites us to consider the emotions that arise as a part of our being in the world. For example, we may experience feelings of desolation when we see a degraded landscape, or we may experience feelings of consolation when we see a flourishing landscape. This discernment becomes an important means to reshape our ecospiritual practices as we participate in rehabilitating degraded landscapes and provide support for maintaining flourishing landscapes.

Ignatius of Loyola enlisted imagination as a means to identify with those people populating the gospel stories. He meant for his spiritual exercises to enable a person to feel at home in Scripture, befriended by Jesus and empowered to live in a quite particular way as a result of this practice. Certainly, our own imaginations can be variously exercised when engaging historical texts about sainted humans and other-than-human ancestors in the faith and when engaging the natural world as our home as sacred text. Discerning the resonance of our own lives within the larger web of life, we are translating spiritual exercise into ecospiritual exercise, habituating our physical lifeways into means of supporting other beings' lives. This ability to discern such resonance is a gift of the imagination and a skill that may be honed. Use of this ability is not a matter of imposing our ego on all parts of the landscape surrounding us, as if we see only ourselves reflected in every facet of life. Rather, use of this ability means we are highly attuned to the interconnections that bind us together with other beings, and in a sense, we reverse the tendency to project our inner landscape outward as we experience ourselves as a reflection of all that is outside us. The transcorporeal identity we share with all creation as bodies housing information and energy that move across materiality allows us to identify with other aspects of creation.

"Spiritual exercises" have been a staple in the history of Christian spiritual practice. Gleaning instructions from the teaching of Jesus formed the basis of early Christian practice—some of which quickly became individual expressions of personal piety rather than the restructuring of unjust relations indicated in some teachings. The idiosyncratic adoption of practice was often elaborated in community and through community attention to marginalized groups of people. Some early monastic experiments, for instance, were based in wealthy widowed women's households and dealt with eliminating social stratification.[17] Some communities formed expressly to address needs of the larger community—becoming centers providing health care, education, and other material goods to redress sickness and poverty.

The earliest monastic communities organized their common life around a recognized leader and a rule of some kind. The rule was legislated, adopted, and revised, with varying degrees of leniency afforded to those who chose to live their lives together by it. We can imagine all sorts of house rules and community agreements that were likely not even discussed among members of a household or community but emerged in the living of life together. We still, of course, live *our* lives governed by spoken and unspoken agreements and social contracts. Marjorie Thompson writes of such legislation as the trellis that supports a plant, mingling our human identity with phytomorphism. She explains:

> Certain kinds of plants need support in order to grow properly. Tomatoes need stakes, and beans much attach themselves to suspended strings. Creeping vines like clematis and wisteria will grow on any structure they can find. Rambling roses take kindly to garden walls, archways, and trellises. Without support, these plants would collapse in a heap on the ground. Their blossoms would not have the space and sun they need to flourish, and their fruits would rot in contact with the soil . . . When it comes to

spiritual growth, human beings are much like these plants. We need structure and support.[18]

"Growth" is so typical a concept for the development of our own lives that we may not think about the creaturely continuity between human and vegetal life that Thompson elaborates, yet it is useful. We do not necessarily anthropomorphize plants but rather reverse our thinking by reminding ourselves that life moves through all parts of creation and that how other-than-human creatures are and act provides meaningful models for our own self-understanding. Further, though some of the supports mentioned in Thompson's description are built supports, some Indigenous peoples speak of the three sisters of corn, beans, and squash as creating a collaborative growing environment that makes possible each plant's flourishing in relationship with the others. The intentionality with which some Indigenous peoples enter relationship with these three plants, helping them create the most opportune setting for mutual support, indicates an important way we, too, might interact with the kin that support our being. We may also interact in mundane ways and in ways typically indicated as spiritual practice.

The thirteenth-century monastic-mystic Gertrude of Helfta used many images of the natural world in her elaboration of spiritual exercises, including a prayer at the conclusion of her work that "the thornbush of [her] heart be converted into . . . a red berry bush of total perfection."[19] Drawing on the monastic setting of her lifeway, Gertrude interpreted initiatory moments of the monastic life—such as rebirth, spiritual conversion, dedication of the self, following of Christ, mystical union, jubilus, and life in death—as moments to elaborate a growing trend to characterize one's commitment in terms resembling human marriage. This spousal love, however, is set aside and possibly even undermined by the beautiful natural imagery Gertrude uses that depicts the divine as the ultimate source of one's sustenance and replenishment. She repeatedly characterizes herself as a kind of dry twig in need of the watering of divine spirit. Her spirit's regenerating and rewilding knits her within the larger web of life that she and her sisters would have shared with the natural world. Ordinary moments of maintaining life together, along with rites of passage associated with the monastic life, are opportunities to experience oneself as continuously reconstituted, like the dry bones of Ezekiel's vision, with divine energies to maintain life. This is what our ecospiritual practice also facilitates as we live more fully into the naturalness we are.

Plants and animals have typically been present in Christian spiritual growth patterns. In iconography, St. George is seen slaying the dragon, a symbol of distractions often unsettlingly associated with the body that draw one's attention from God and others. St. Francis spoke of his body and of restraining its desires as subduing "brother ass." Even in the Zen Buddhist tradition, we see in the Ox-Herding Pictures scenes of domestication in which an animal (the anima, or soul) is tamed. The harshness toward the self that these pictures depict gives rise to an insensibility toward the body and toward the literal animal used as symbol. Cruelty toward animals is thus tolerated when exercised as a means to elaborate oneself as uniquely other-than-animal. That the Christian spiritual tradition also has so much room for this kind of cruelty should give us pause and require us to find and create new imagery of the human spiritual life. If we are to continue using animals symbolically, we should do so positively in order to rehabilitate our attitude toward both the human body and toward the animal kin with whom we share life.

A counterbalance might be attributed to Melangell of Powys, a sixth-century monastic woman. Legend states that she protected a hare pursued by a prince's hunting dogs and that the prince granted her land to use as a refuge for all who seek safety.[20] The physicality of her embodied and enclothed presence that allowed the hare to boldly face and then even repel the dogs suggests a transcorporeal connection with land that, in the legend, is designated a "perpetual asylum," within which the vulnerable might grow their own resilience. The legend tells that upon receipt of land to be made such a refuge, Melangell was continuously surrounded by hares cavorting as tamed, domesticated creatures. I wonder if another aspect of this legend might be that Melangell's rewilded being, emergent from many years in contemplative silence alone on the land prior to being discovered, was recognized and celebrated by other wild creatures in the Welsh countryside. Perhaps another version of this legend exists in hare communities, a story of the human who once lived as they did—in a thicket of brambles, large and full of thorns—as our human story tells us and who put her body between the hunter and the prey.

The artist Marcy Hall has created a lovely icon of Melangell holding a hare and hiding another in the folds of her gown, with the inscription, "Take the soft hare of your life in your arms." What a powerfully transformative sensibility this instruction, gleaned from the spirit of Melangell's story, expresses! While the legend does not seem explicit about this connection of human and hare life, the archaeologist Caroline Malim explains the pre-Christian context of this legend and the place where it originated:

> Hares are predominantly nocturnal and closely linked to the moon goddess in legends around the world. Sometimes the hare is the goddess herself in disguise, and sometimes it [the hare] is her messenger . . . The eating of hare meat was taboo in some cultural traditions, due in no small part to the belief that women, witches and the moon goddess would shape shift into the form of a hare (as can some shamans). For example, in Kerry, Ireland, the eating of hare meat was likened to eating one's own grandmother.[21]

The long and short of it is that the way we treat animals is reflected in our treatment of other humans and ourselves and vice versa. Discerning this connection in our lives helps us change our thinking, our language, and our behavior. Our imaginations may not seem to be trained in this direction. However, many ecofeminists have pointed out the routine use of language to speak of animals to speak of women in derogatory ways. "The Life of Melangell" suggests that ecospiritual practice and ecospiritual exercises might recalibrate human presence across scale, as protector of the vulnerable and as one who realizes their own protected status in a particular place or how habitat protects them generously.

We human beings seem to have a lot of curiosity about the mystery that is our lives and about the mysteries that surround us. While it is easy for us to also divert ourselves from essential sources of satisfaction for our curiosity, the narrativizing desire of our brain function might account for our absorption in other people's stories. Our curiosity is somewhat sated there. Thus, we might binge-watch a Netflix series as a way of entering another world, escaping our own for a bit; get caught up in the Humans of New York social media presence, which offers glimpses of other people's lives; or lose all track of time when absorbed in a really good novel. None of this is wrong, entirely, but I wonder to what degree our distractions within the narrative worlds of others account for the devastations our cultural, social, and ecological worlds are experiencing right now? And I wonder whether some repair work might be effected by and within the narrative worlds of others as we reconfigure our imaginations to behold what is constantly happening around and inclusive of us. Some of the stories archived by the Imagine 2200 project hold mesmerizing visions of an abundant shared future that, I imagine, were told to catalyze movement toward those particular possibilities.[22]

Ironically, my own attention to this absorption with the narratives of others was stoked by a sci-fi series, a spinoff of *Star Trek* in which the Denobulan doctor, Phlox, expresses intrigue at the human characters' enjoyment of watching a classic film. He comments that his own species had thrown off such habits long ago, having recovered the pleasure of attending to their *own* stories. I wonder if we, too, might return to the pleasure of our own stories and the sharing of them, in person as we are able, given the exigencies of our times. These stories include both the apocalyptic stories that function as a release mechanism for the distress we experience during an ongoing real-life ecoapocalypse and stories about humans creatively adapting to climate change, responsive to the needs of others (human and more-than-human). For me, sometimes, it can be difficult to reengage older stories that once enthralled me because now I really feel the lack of their characters' sensibility of something as pressing in my world as climate change, racial reckoning, and transformation of our economic and class systems. I wonder if this time requires that we shape and value new narratives, new kinds of (s)heroism, and new expressions of possibilities of interspecies life that will help us to challenge the status quo, some elements of which we recognize and some of which we don't (yet).

Though I tend to focus on practice as a name for the organizing activities of our time and as being *formative* in the field of Christian spirituality, there are other means just as important. We would do well to regard these as transformative means, especially as they are rewilded. These other organizing means are ceremony, ritual, therapy, and play. Intersecting with practice, these other means of forming and transforming our experience have their peculiar traits that help us reach full-bodied awareness and enjoyment of our lives as ecospiritual beings. They aren't a luxury. They aren't just for those who are privileged with excess in the form of time or money. Rather, they are an essential component of our human experience. These ways of defining ourselves as human beings with and for one another are a right for everybody. They remind us that we exist beyond our identification within a militaristic-capitalist empire.

Indigenous ethnobotanist Robin Wall Kimmerer defines ceremony as a "vehicle for belonging—to a family, to a people, and to the land."[23] We may think of marriage ceremonies or citizenship ceremonies as particular events that help to realize the relationships of belonging that are forming between people. Significantly, Kimmerer describes an inadvertent kind of ceremony her father used to perform when the family was camping that consisted of offering the first cup of coffee of the day to the land. That this happened at the opening of the day was a significant gesture. Its influence remained with Kimmerer throughout the day, as many people's morning routines do, especially when they are ceremonious in nature—that is, intentional about operating as Kimmerer describes a ceremony might, as a vehicle for belonging. Over time, Kimmerer learned there was a practical reason why her father poured out this first cup; it rid the rest of the pot of some of the grounds they didn't want to drink. I love this little detail that shows how even practical needs that we have may become ceremony when they foster belonging, as Kimmerer experienced in belonging with her family on the land during these camping trips. She claims the power of ceremony is that "it marries the mundane to the sacred."[24] We might then consider that meeting our own everyday needs can constitute ceremony. Meeting our needs for food when growing, procuring, or preparing food with and for others can be ceremony. Meeting our needs for physical exercise when hiking, biking, or kayaking can be ceremony.

Another way spirituality may inform our commitments to being intentional about transformation, personal and collective, is through ritual. Ritualist Francis Weller defines ritual as "any gesture done with emotion and intention by an individual or a group that attempts to connect the individual or the community with transpersonal energies for the purposes of healing and transformation."[25] A well-crafted ritual can be cathartic in allowing a participant to express and release pain and suffering. Rituals can mark rites of passage through important transitions, initiating a person into the challenges and joys of a new identity. Though some people are noting the lack of cultural ritual in withdrawal from formal religious spaces, there persists a yearning for it among many and curiosity about the needs rituals address; further, many are using their creativity to imagine and adopt rituals that answer persistent needs.

Sometimes ritual can be formed on the fly when, for instance, a person is invited to make a simple gesture of gratitude for time together with others or outside or invited to make an offering of beauty to a place that's been devastated. My own experimentation with ritual in the outdoors occurred a few seasons ago when I was nursing trauma from a professional boundary that had been violated. I was at the coast, and I realized I needed a ritual of some kind to provide closure to the months of reflection on what had happened, even as I realized that the trauma would persist in my body and psyche for a while to come. I took some ice cubes from the ice machine in the motel where I was staying and went out to sit safely on the rocks above the waves that were crashing around me. When ready, I slipped each ice cube into the water, offering them as symbols of the hurt I carried and wishing to effect an inner dissolving of the hurt just as the ocean would dissolve the ice, taking the water back into itself. This did effect a meaningful change for me, though it operated in a one-way fashion in that nothing I was doing helped the ocean or waters more generally.

While ritual is a name for a formal process to catalyze healing, therapy also relates to healing. Therapy is a healing modality that emerges from repeated effort, much like practice. Its principal objective is the uncovering of wounds, suffering, and trauma to understand one's story about these aspects of human experience and to begin healing through this attention. Using therapy often involves another person who can function as healer, whose expertise, witnessing, listening, and guidance can be crucial to the success of healing. When oriented toward the goal of healing, however, therapy can be ongoing; many aspects of human life can involve retraumatization, rendering the feasibility of complete healing an open question. New therapeutic modalities express recognition that the "wounded healer" can enhance the possibility of mutuality in healing between therapist and patient, while other new modalities also involve nature and the recognition that in the form of a particular landscape and place, it can offer space in which to understand one's belonging and meaning. Ecotherapy as applied ecopsychology takes insights about the healing of mind to the restorative relationship that can form when a person is outdoors. Many scientific studies report on the efficacy of exposure to real and even perceived nature, the latter being accessed through pictures or indoor surroundings enhanced by colors of the natural landscape. We may be able to learn more about how our disconnection from the natural world impacts our healing and how restoring this relationship produces well-being.

Nature's efficacy in healing also leads to the role of play in the ecospiritual life. While I don't see a patient in a hospital bed thinking of their experience of healing being promoted by a picture of a forest or ocean on the wall, there is a sense in which the body/mind complex is willingly deceived into responding favorably given just the semblance of an optimal environment. That we can function in this way as human beings may constitute a species gift we should play with more often, if not at the expense of our so-called *real* experiences of nature. I hesitate to examine this tendency too closely for it may seem to promote virtual reality and the way we consume nature through taking photographs to share through social media and provide others with vicarious means of engaging the natural world. *And* that we do this so habitually, often marveling enviously at others' outdoor escapades, explains in part our addiction to social media.

Play, however, occupies a mundane role in our lives that can be engaged for transformation as it lets us release our preoccupations with who or how we are supposed to be and allows us to step into or deepen our creativity and the possibilities that life offers us. Greening Michel Foucault's technologies of the self, for instance, we might think of play as a deliberate calling into question of our various societal identities and roles. Activating our potential to be plural, we can assume authority and expertise in places where we may not be recognized for this. As scholar-practitioners, some of us may engage imposter syndrome in ourselves and others, and we may, to effect our healing and transformation, need to productively engage this tendency to move past the strictures it places on our activities. We cannot afford to be paralyzed by doubt or fear of mistakes at this time in our human history; rather, we need every experiment in life that can be catalyzed to make lots of mistakes so that we move into greater capacity to create the abundant futures we want.

Engaging habits of ceremony, ritual, therapy, and play in our everyday lives, we recreate our traditional modes of being with God, with one another, with ourselves, and with the natural world. We consider how our typical spiritual practices might look when sourcing our vital need to grow curious about and responsive to the impacts we have in this world, as an individual and as a member of a faith community or educational space. As we grow our skill to think and act creatively, we also grow the courage to face what is difficult about growing the worlds we can imagine, facing our own internal obstacles while also negotiating what is limiting (legitimately and otherwise) in the world around us. Humility might be a watchword for this enterprise, connecting us etymologically as well as phenomenologically with our being earth—humus—and behaving accordingly. Adapting our humanness to match the needs of our communities of faith and our larger communities of the beloved Earth, we may pray with Cláudio Carvalhaes:

> Our God who art in pluriverses, the skies and the earth,
>
> Blessed be your name: life. May your pulsing life come to be seen, heard, touched, and felt through the oceans, the forests, in the rocks, in the life of plants and in the sounds of animals and singing birds.
>
> May the atmosphere of the sky that carries our ability to breathe stay balanced as fossils are kept under the earth.
>
> Give us this day our daily bread through a variety of seeds and grains and leaves without pesticides, without monocultures, from local farms and agro-biodiverse-cultures.
>
> Forgive our plundering of the earth, our total lack of relation and reciprocity with the earth and more than human beings; as cells, mycelium, fungi and infinite processes of symbiosis forgive us daily by giving life back when we destroy it.
>
> And lead us not into consumerism and devouring the earth but deliver us from the apathy that says nothing can be changed.
>
> For life is kinship, relationally and reciprocity. Now and forever.
>
> *Amen.*[26]

ECOSPIRITUAL KINSHIP PRACTICE: TERRASPIRITUAL INQUIRY

Grow curious about your needs and where they originate. Are they truly yours, or are they what you've been told you're entitled to or should desire? A premise of this book is that you need a certain amount of wildness in your life; adjudicate that premise. Do you think it's true for you, and if so, how much wildness is necessary for you? Where is wildness lacking in your life now? Where might wildness be struggling to spring forth, like a weed or root through a crack of concrete, and where might you tenderly turn your attention and let that part of your life grow bolder and stronger, breaking up the places that make its emergence difficult?

In the area of ecopsychology and its applied form, ecotherapy, Craig Chalquist has elaborated a methodology called terrapsychological inquiry to address how a specific place interacts meaningfully in informing one's understanding and insights related to place and to the people and other creature kin who inhabit and compose such a place. Chalquist explains that terrapsychology "is the field of imaginative studies, ideas, and practices for restorying and thereby reenchanting our relations with the world, with each other and with ourselves."[27] Terrapsychological inquiry starts with the premise that psyche is "larger" or more comprehensive than that possessed or experienced just by humans. *Psyche* is a name for the energy of information moving through a place and expressed in various material forms.

Similarly, the ancient notion of anima mundi, or spirit of a place, animates the translation of terrapsychological inquiry into *terraspiritual inquiry*. This translation occurs as we listen to the spirit of a place, allowing our dreams, emotions, and empathic identifications with others—and our reversals of assumptions about fixed form—to shape our identities and the ecospiritual practices we adopt. In the sense I present it here, terraspiritual inquiry is a means of developing capacity to discern what the spirit of a place expresses and thus means; this practice is akin to the kind of prayer that is more a listening-to than a talking-to.

To assume a posture of terraspiritual inquiry, tend not only to the voice of the outdoors, listening for what the patterns of creaturely life around you express. Listen as well to the voice of your dreams. Some ecotherapists even advise asking Earth for a message through one's dreams before one goes to bed. What do I need to know? What does my place need or want me to know? Be prepared to regard your dreams as an answer. Keeping a notebook can help you record impressions as you wake or recall images and actions from your dreams. Certainly, conversation with a spiritual director or therapist can help with dream interpretation as well. This practice helps you begin to regard your unconscious as part of the terrain of life you share with all creaturely kin, an important dimension of your inner ecology. Desire, loss, struggle, and enthusiasm all move in language-free ways of felt contact between you and others of our world, and responsible discernment and use of these messages require wise practice.

As you cultivate an attitude of regarding yourself as aware of and interested in the life of the world around you, you will notice more. This back-and-forth, and the modifying of your life in response to what you discern, constitutes a kind of prayer. As Origen of Alexandria wrote so long ago in a treatise on prayer, we could aim to make all our life one long prayer. Greening or rewilding this teaching means transforming our theocentric focus to include the multiple ways God may be experienced through creation. This can happen more readily when we experience terraspiritual inquiry as a mode of learning from and responding to the realities of our creature kin. This kind of prayer practice just might lead us to other forms of active and contemplative prayer and to fusions of the two that transform our inner worlds as well as the social and ecological systems we form part of.

CHAPTER FOUR

Sacred Kinship

Contemplation—Mystery—Geophany

She Who Cherishes Our Hot Mess . . . Immanence is Her Jam.[1]

The sacred wild is the site of kinship expression. What do I mean by this? The sacred wild is the site of what we most value, though we might not often act in ways that convince us we know this sacred wild is valuable. "God" is a tricky name with which to maneuver in this space of identifying and honoring the sacred wild. Because the name carries so much baggage for religious and nonreligious people alike, we may avoid associating it with what we experience in the outdoors, as if what theologian and activist Christena Cleveland calls the whitemalegod could be offended by this merger with material creation. I've chosen in this chapter to regard the sacred as an opening to the figures we have used, as individuals and communities, to think about our ultimate source. This generative source hosts the creative powers that gave and give birth to the world. The energies and powers of this generative source divinely persist through everything that is. To simply speak of "this" as God feels inadequate and reductive yet is a portal to the depth experience of life in which *God, Creator, source, divine presence*, and the *sacred* are all terms to indicate what is irrepressibly present and alive. To consider this dimension of our human experience as *cherishing* our "hot mess" is a welcome reassurance from Cleveland that I'll try to live into in this chapter. My main concern is to play around with the immanence dimension of God that is always present to, with, and through us as a necessary quality of reconstituting our kinship relations with all creaturekind. And while God language may not be the best to work with for all readers, I'll try to use various qualities often attributed to God to speak to the sacred a bit more broadly, especially as this constitutes a kinship between ourselves and other species with whom we share our planetary home. Could *God* somehow be used to refer to these relationships, too, in the sense of how some are theorizing a creaturely embodiment of God with words like *divinanimality* (hybridizing the divine and the animal as conceptual, theorized "others" of the human) and *ecotherology* (*eco* meaning home, *thero* meaning beast, and *logy* meaning word or discourse)?[2]

As a species, we seem to favor forming specialized language to speak of the reality that surrounds and sustains us, that causes us both to marvel and to grow intimate with, a dimension of *what is* that feminist post-Christian philosopher Daphne Hampson characterized as "that through which we come to be most fully ourselves."[3] Hampson's definition helps us realize the material nature of this reality quite fully: we certainly could not come to be any measure of ourselves without the air we breathe, the food we consume, the shelter we inhabit, and the radical belonging we experience as members of the Earth community. Ecophilosopher David Abram refers to a *corporeal faith* when designating these material means that give rise to human consciousness and the possibility of deepening our relationship with others.[4] Whatever it is that threads through these quite tangible realities of our human existence also sustains our being and sparks our awareness of unknown dimensions of ourselves. We may always have things about our existence that remain mysterious and unknown, but these things need not be regarded as immaterial for that reason.

For now, without adequate language or understanding to engage these things, we use words like *the sacred, the transcendent, the divine, the holy, the unknown, the mystery,* and many other such names that draw us, too often, out of the rootedness of experience with material reality. I wonder if we are yet so uncertain of our origins, identity, and purpose that we long for something "beyond" to answer to and draw into our relations, like a marker anchored elsewhere but enabling a web to form. God, then, can be a useful concept to think with that organizes and gives meaning to our lives but which we nevertheless too often assume belongs more appropriately "elsewhere" than within our midst. For such a hubristic species, we are unaccountably humble about this aspect of ourselves. Yet, attempting to account for this humility, we might also acknowledge that our tendency to locate the divine outside our midst has allowed people with power to maintain their power. They use their authority to help the rest of us find and access the holy in exchange for our awe at their power and our readiness to accept and maintain it.

The parable of the twelfth camel, retold by Donna Haraway in her *Staying with the Trouble*, illuminates the paradoxical quality of needing to borrow concepts with which to think and our capacity to do so. In a chapter on scholarship and world-making as a practice of curiosity, she tells the story of a man who left his three sons a "seemingly impossible inheritance" of eleven camels that were to be apportioned to each son in a specific way: the eldest to receive half, the second to receive a quarter, and the youngest to receive a sixth. Obviously, eleven camels cannot be divided in such a way, and the story goes on to explain:

> The perverse requirements of the legacy provoked the confused sons, who were on the verge of failing to fulfill the terms of the will, to visit an old man living in the village. His savvy kindness in giving the sons a twelfth camel allowed the heirs to create a solution to their difficult heritage; they could make their inheritance active, alive, generative. With twelve camels, the fractions worked, and there was one camel left over to give back to the old man.[5]

The math involved in this story is delightfully paradoxical and yet so simple. My choice to place the tale in this chapter on the sacred reveals something of how I think of God and the host of words that crystalize around "God" as a shareable offering enabling us to work with "it" and then release "it." There is no need to hold on to the offering once "it" has done its job in allowing us to organize everything else around it. While it might sound like this story works as a metaphor for the transcendent—something from outside the system that comes within to activate or catalyze change—the parable underscores the commonality between shared systems. Haraway, a significant transdisciplinary scholar and philosopher of science, inherited this story from disciplinary colleague Vinciane Despret, who passed it on from Isabelle Stengers. The borrowing of concepts to provisionally hold space for possibilities to unfold is what this story is all about, and the camels represent a common species—the "borrowed" camel not occupying fundamentally different existential qualities from the herd it was introduced to. What this story helps me think of is the radical invitation to celebrate our material reality as the means by which anything God might be conceived and known. The rootedness of our meaning-making and values-affirming work in the material universe would go a long way toward effecting repair of the ecological damage we have already done as a species.

If we are to rewild *Spirit* in particular, and to understand the ways that Spirit enables our kinship relations, it also makes sense to use this kind of parable. That spirituality differs from theology is important. For some Christian spirituality scholars, the field has operated as a kind of corrective to breathe new life into what theology was supposed to have always been about: the encounter with God. As the desert Christian Evagrius claimed, "If you are a theologian you truly pray. If you truly pray you are a theologian."[6] This ancient notion of what it meant to be a theologian has seemed to some to decay over time as systematic study and theorizing about God took the place of encounter and relationship. To revivify the encounter and do this corrective work could spell the end of the need for "spirituality studies" per se. Yet so much corrective work is happening that the momentum of the field's creation has taken on a life of its own as a site of interspiritual practice and companioning in a way that differs methodologically from interreligious dialogue and comparative studies. That *spirituality*, a word rooted in the experience of living beings, might help us rethink the categories, definitions, and explanations offered by theology is an important aspect of the discipline's work.

The origin of the word and idea of *spirituality* harken back to breath itself, without which we could not survive. We cannot *hold onto* our breath and survive. Similarly, the temporary holding of something so fundamentally other and yet bound to and with us enables us to function and understand ourselves as coconstituting with breath and all who share breath. David Abram speculates that God's name in the Hebrew text, the unspoken yet breathed and breathable tetragrammaton, fleshes out the reality of our material vulnerability regarding air and our tendency to thus use air fundamentally to express God's very name. At Reed College here in Portland, I have witnessed Abram perform his spectacular weaving of God's name with breathing, and it is a miraculous aural introduction to this amazing insight into relating God's name with the material dependence on air we all share. Certainly, we have not always been the breathing creatures we are now. With climate change, there may come a time when our species adaptations require us to breathe in new ways or to engage our material sustenance in a different way to support our living. I imagine at that time new imagery for the *Spirit* and for the sacred will emerge.

CONTEMPLATING BURNING BUSHES

Pope Francis describes Christian spirituality in his 2015 encyclical *Laudato Si'* as "proposing an alternative understanding to the quality of life, and encourage[ing] a prophetic and *contemplative* lifestyle, one capable of deep enjoyment free of obsession with consumption." He goes on to advocate that we learn to be "present to each reality" and that we grow the "capacity to be happy with little" and grateful.[7]

In other words, we move to a renewed sense of what it means to be human, in effect, in ways that resonate with our ancestral experience. We haven't always lived in ways requiring our thoughtless rushing from one task to another. We haven't always lived in ways that don't allow us to take notice of what and who are around us, to contemplate the world we belong to and to contemplate our interior landscape as resonant with that world. We haven't always lived separated from the sources of our true creativity, pleasure, and even intelligence. Once upon a time, we may nostalgically muse, we had the opportunity to evolve in ways more respectful and reflective of our natural environment and creature kin. Once upon a time, we chose to live more closely with the beings who coconstitute our lives and who depend on us as well.

The origins of contemplative practice are ancient and emerge from many different contexts, all expressing a people's consciousness of the governance of the natural world and how the human community is formed in response to that governance. Contemplation is the art of discernment by pausing and attending to what is seen, heard, or felt, almost by means of a mysterious sixth sense. You may notice that the word *contemplation* shares its heart with temple—that is, contemplation is about making sacred space, as a temple, within which the sacred might be heard and attended to and whose guidance may be evoked and followed. Today, contemplation typically means slowing down and pausing. It can mean mindfulness. It can be attached to a number of other activities, all signaling a specific approach to performing these activities that entails intention and attention. The sacred may or may not be explicitly involved, yet the elaboration of a kinship relation through listening to messages communicated through our natural world constitutes its own type of sacred encounter.

One form of ancient contemplative practice that enables people to create space for discernment was use of a Chinese oracle bone. The bone might have had carved lines on it that generated meaning when, having landed in a particular way, lines were visible, invisible, or pointing in certain directions. Similarly, practitioners in other cultures might throw twigs or stones within a sacred circle or demarcated space in which their landing position would "speak" certain messages that a diviner could interpret and enact. Though ancestral or other spirits might sometimes be thought responsible for the movement of the divinatory tool, those engaging in this practice also understood that forces beyond their understanding—both natural and supernatural—were involved. We may have the sophistication to call these forces gravity, electromagnetism, or wind currents, but the recognition of reliance on the actions of Earth others suggested by these ancient practices schools us in our ongoing reliance on them. Similarly, birds flying within a certain range might mediate a message or guidance facilitated by the wind currents and the volition of the bird's life energies that yield a particular message for the perceptive discerner. To return to the material in the introduction of this book about greening hermeneutics, this ancient divinatory process recalls a radical commitment to understanding the natural world as mediating all important, valued messages. The process of understanding those messages requires a person to trust that the way the world works has potential to yield meaning.

I remember first learning, as a piano student, about John Cage's strange work and feeling bewildered by the novelty of his composition 4'33, literally four minutes and thirty-three seconds of silence. Performing the piece, a pianist (or perhaps another instrumentalist or singer) occupies the stage in silence; the sounds of the venue become the performance. I imagine this composition as a kind of "twelfth camel" loaned to the music-loving community to help its members sense more deeply their own embeddedness within and participation in creating a richly aural landscape. Similarly, as Cage created setups such as a piano with an aquarium of fish indicating which musical notes should be played, he called our attention to the unique temporality of all creation, *cosmogenesis*. All is beginning, coming into being, and emergent and disappearing in various stages and overlapping and impinging on one another. We come to know and experience within this ebbing and flowing world.

An animal rights advocate might cringe at the use of animal life of this kind, but these activities of discernment also cultivate deep recognition that so much of our life as a species has been determined or formed in relation to the natural world already. So little of our life as a species has been constituted by relationships with automated processes, human-built environments, and machines. Unlike a biblical figure like Moses, who encountered the holy at a burning bush (Exod 3), we more readily engage screens and digital realities to mediate our messages from the often-remote human world. Moses's encounter was significant in forming a whole community. Moses was told to remove his shoes, and he stood with no human-made artifact to bar his bodily contact with Earth. In similarly removing his doubt and his avoidance of the injustice he had fled in Egypt, he was recalled to his senses through his curiosity at the bush that burned but was not consumed. Obviously, there is a disjunction between the biblical vehicle of theophany in the unconsumed burning bush and the reality we share today, when so many trees, animals, and habitats are consumed by wildfire. How to reconcile this disjunction? Or rather, how to rewild this disjunction? After all, the book of Hebrews contains the claim that God is a *consuming* fire (Heb 12:29). What does that mean for us in a world of anthropogenic climate change? What messages do our burning forests relay to us if we are listening?

We cannot quickly move to making the divine being one who burns away our impurities as the refiner's fire (Mal 3:2), rendering us more equipped to be in the presence of God as perhaps Moses's removal of sandals indicates. However, acknowledging the metaphorical possibilities suggested by fire as indicative of divine life, the inspiration of divine being within us and to which we are responsive, does reinforce the interconnectedness we share with all creation. Rather than regarding ourselves as the pattern imposed on the rest of creation in iterative and lesser forms, we might think instead with resonance as our working principle. The shimmering of identities and experiences that differ from and resemble each other simultaneously and at different times, scales, and places suggests the radical connectedness that deifies our life by virtue of its participation in this web of life and that sacralizes all that is. Using resonance as our working principle, we might see human life as derivative from others and turn the tables on our default perceptions that image other parts of creation through our self-understandings of identity and experience.

We might think of the consuming here as happening in a very material manner in our world today. Consider the real, living arboreal and other beings whose lives are charred almost beyond recognition by the devastating fire that moves through them on an annual, and sometimes more often, basis. If we expand our recognition of sacred space to contain these vulnerable places of creation and to witness the burning of trees, bushes, and animal life and the vanishing of creeks, rivers, and streams, we may contemplatively engage this phenomenon of the forest fire for the message it conveys and the guidance it provides. The world is being consumed as collateral damage from our unjust actions. We are often indifferent to the impact we have on creation when we don't see the impact or spend time reflecting on the relationship we have with it. We don't let ourselves be too close to the suffering for fear of what we may feel. Ecotheologian Sallie McFague justly calls this aspect of our natural world's suffering *crucifixion*,[8] aligning it with the interhuman oppression so characteristic of our species for so long. This aligning should startle us into recognizing our complicity in the injustice causing suffering throughout the natural world and should register our desire to contribute to a resurrection of life within crucified spaces. This contribution to transfiguration is sacred work and draws our own being into the caretaking, mutual aid, and radical kinship our species is capable of. Macrina Wiederkehr reminds us:

> To be [a] child of wonder you must learn to take off your shoes often. Taking off your shoes is a sacred ritual. It is a hallowed moment of remembering the goodness of space and time. It is a way of celebrating the holy ground on which you stand. If you want to be a child of wonder cherish the truth that time and space are holy. Whether you take off your shoes symbolically

> or literally matters little. What is important is that you are alive to the holy ground on which you stand and to *the holy ground that you are.*[9]

This urging us to consider ourselves in creaturely continuity with the holy ground upon which we move helps us take on the difficult work of tending to the earth and to seeing that it is also a tending to our own need for healing. Wiederkehr claims the symbolism or literalism of shoe removal doesn't matter; I would suggest that it does. Insofar as we're able, our felt contact with the world of which we're a part should be cultivated and celebrated. It matters that we are able to make contact materially through our skin, whether the soles of our feet or elsewhere on the body, touching the world that sustains us and to sense the vital exchange that happens. This felt contact may not always be pleasant; the transcorporeal connection we share means we let in the toxins we allow to proliferate in the world. Nevertheless, we need to find simple, accessible ways to refresh and maintain this contact, despite the pleasure or the pain. For lack of this contact, we damage ourselves and others. This then becomes work of personal healing and of justice.

GEOPHANY AND A SACRED UNIVERSE

The "God-question," as one of my colleagues puts it, seems to capture the imaginations of many today, especially when scientific discoveries lead to diverging responses among scientists and the layperson of both affirming God's creativity and eliminating the need for a God of the gaps. While the concept of deep incarnation helps Christians understand how our material universe is thoroughly saturated with divine presence, our categories of immanence and transcendence operate in so binary a fashion as to make it difficult to conceive of who God may really be for us. In my work, "the sacred" has become an important functional category of human experience that can hold both immanence and transcendence. The category effectively ties spirituality more closely to religion, through experience, rather than to theology, which has to do more with thorough-going reflection on our experience. When we opt to consider things sacred, however, other things necessarily become not sacred, and that kind of bifurcation even of our material, embodied experience has become increasingly troublesome to me. I sometimes use the idea of animation when thinking through the sacred, thinking that what has been considered soul (anima) is the animating power in living being. While that is a sacred quality of life, perhaps the simple reason that it is animating constitutes its real value. We value and can consider sacred that which animates our lives. The resurgence and renewed valuation of animism in contemporary thought affirms this bypassing of God-language or God-ideas to align the sacred, the spiritual, and the soulful with what is essentially animating and animated. For animists, even what appears most inanimate can nevertheless be inspirited and in relation with other inspirited beings.

I have sometimes considered myself a radical empiricist. I believe our categories of immaterial and material to consider the spirit/soul/animating power that gives and sustains life and the bodies of our physical world are too binary, too reductionistic, and too logic-seeking to ultimately please. I tend to think that all reality is material and that its intangible pieces are still material, just immeasurable by any standards or equipment we currently have to ascertain them. It may never be the case that we have such capabilities, and that is fine with me. Instead, it behooves us to live into a radical trust that what is real is of multiple kinds—seen and unseen, touchable and untouchable—even what/whom we have been used to call "God." In considering our own experience, it has seemed that God might even want to be identified as being intimate with our experience, not observing from without. And while the multiverse hypothesis speaks to the idea that some larger matrix exists where inaccessible parallel worlds arise, much as soap bubbles in the popular image, that matrix still carries all the associations of something beyond our material world that we can only intuit.

Geophany and the notion of deep incarnation can provide a remedy to unsettling dislocations of our sense of the sacred as emergent outside our known worlds. The latter notion refers to what some ecotheologians have begun to use as a framework for considering, in the Christian tradition, the implications of God's taking form in not just a human body but also in the materiality of the universe. Thus, immanence and transcendence may persist as meaningful distinctions but only within the context of the material world. As Mark Hathaway and Leonardo Boff put it:

> Our solar system, the Earth, and each being and person, contain recycled material from these stars that were released into the wider cosmos through supernova explosions. The body of Jesus . . . possessed this same ancestral origins and was made from the cosmic dust birthed in the interior of ancient stars that long predated our planet and solar system. The iron that ran through his veins, the phosphorus and calcium that fortified his bones, the sodium and potassium that facilitated the transmission of signals through his nerves, the oxygen that made up 65 percent of his body and the carbon that made up an additional 18 percent—all of this makes the incarnation a truly cosmic event.[10]

The shared materiality through the body of Jesus, to which all parts of creation are privy, helps us highlight the nature of our radical kinship with all aspects of creation. The emergence of a Christ figure within other species and for other purposes, to engage with the members of the world formed by that species, is definitely beyond our understanding. Yet our querying of anthropocentrism in even our Christology may make it necessary to consider the variations of ways incarnation, deep and otherwise, occur in multiple fashion, temporally and spatially.

Related to theophany, which describes the manifestation of God (as, for instance, with the story of the burning bush), geophany evokes the manifestation of Earth, of land, of something related very much to this world we all share. Geophany means a sudden recognition of the vitality and strangeness of a place that has perhaps become so familiar to us that we do not even see it anymore, as the sudden emergence of divinity can disrupt all preconceptions of localizing a god. Tim Robinson wrote tellingly of geophany to evoke consciousness of how particular places manifest themselves when we are attentive to them, riveted perhaps as Moses was by the burning bush appearing at the periphery of his task of tending sheep. Transforming in part his work as *geology* to *geophany*, Robinson reflected on offering new language to express a sensibility born of his deep engagement with place:

> Enquiring out placenames, mapping, has become for me not a way of making a living or making a career, but of making a life; a mode of dwelling in a place. In composing each of the placename instances I have given you into a brief epiphany, a showing forth of the nature of the place, I am suggesting that what is hidden from us is not something rare and occult, or even augustly sacred, but, too often, the Earth we stand on. I present to you a new word: "geophany." A theophany is a showing forth, the manifestation, of God, or of a god; geophany therefore must be the showing forth of the Earth.
>
> In the west of Ireland there is a language and a place lore uniquely fitted to the geophany of that land, with its skies full of migrating alphabets, waves that conspire to lift the currach ashore, its mountains like teeming udders, its foot-chilling bogs, the donkey's bray of its history, its ancient words piled on hilltops. My work is possible thanks to what I have grasped of the geophanic language of Ireland. My work thanks that language.[11]

The connection between geophany and deep incarnation we might elaborate as part of a Christian ecospirituality enhances our understanding that something significant happens through the Earth body we are part of when we notice. The flaring forth that draws our recognition can come forth through beauty and that which we deeply appreciate about the world. A similar idea is resonant in the Celtic Christian tradition associated with "thin places," where a kind of veil over a landscape may thin so that we see its real sacredness. This place can operate as a kind of portal between immanence and transcendence, seeming to unite them in liminal space. Awakening to the reality that all places have this potential, we may express greater care in attending to geophanies in the world around us. In addition to manifestations of place through beauty, we can also have our notice of a place heightened through our grief over the suffering and dying we witness in landscapes, habitats, species, and creature kin all around us. The call to liberation that such geophanies can occasion for us equips us to more readily pause, attend, and listen to the deep cries of solidarity within our own experience and then to engage the work needed to initiate and continue repair and healing.

Deepening our notion of the body of God—language that Sallie McFague introduced us to decades ago in her *Models of God: Theology for an Ecological, Nuclear Age*,[12] we sense that even our celebrations, whether daily or weekly Eucharistic celebrations or other liturgies in which God's body is present, must reckon with so many more possibilities. We can broaden the liturgical season to work in our recognition of the diverse ways geophanies express recognition of radical kinship with all our creature kin, and we can inaugurate new outdoor liturgies that have us feasting and giving thanks for the kinship relations that sustain us. The forest therapy practice emergent in some contexts in the past few years includes a ritual tea ceremony in which participants partake of tea brewed from elements of the forest that has just provided a therapeutic setting for engagement. This drawing into our bodies with intention and ceremony elements that always source and sustain us helps us become more responsible for the world we share with others.

The Cistercian monk and reviver of centering prayer practice, Thomas Keating, wrote, "When the presence of God emerges from our inmost being into our faculties, whether we walk down the street or drink a cup of soup, divine life is pouring into the world."[13] This emergence from within aligns with the sense of incarnation that

God's body in the person of Christ sanctified all human bodies. To regard our own bodies as a source of this divine indwelling in the material universe is a particular gift of Christianity to our contemporary ecological crisis. By deepening our incarnational theology to include all matter, we see how it is possible that divine life is pouring into and emergent from within all that exists in the world. The marvelous and the mundane are kin. Transcendence and immanence themselves are kin.

MOUNTAIN GEOPHANIES

Among some of the desert Christians, the notion that God might be imaged at all was heretical, and in the late 300s, there was a disturbance among some of the desert Christians in Egypt that resulted in endings of viable communities. We have some fragments of this history, though most of the sayings collections feature very little that is of a doctrinal nature. We get brief snippets of doctrine, as in a saying attributed to Athanasius (an ascetic bishop whose ecclesial commitments allowed him to stay and learn with the desert Christians) that "Jesus is equal to God in the same way that one seeing is accomplished with two eyes."[14]

Most desert sayings focus on the experiential, the learned wisdom useful to be shared with others. Cultivating a relationship with God was among those practical "things" taught, and the desert Christians influenced by Origenist thought endeavored to be very careful about how they attuned their senses to an imaged God. For them, God had to be regarded and experienced as wholly transcendent. In part, we can see the sensibility embedded in this regard and experience. It serves to safeguard what they presumed God needed safeguarding against: human presumption. That we might be able to say definitively who or what God is made the desert Christians feel a bit like the Israelites in worshipping a golden calf (Exod 32). These ancestors in faith and those who saved their stories seemed to have been concerned about how much their worship resembled the worship of other peoples and to have sought a means to differentiate themselves from others and their God from others' gods. This need resonated in the first centuries of Christianity as theorists of this faith sought concepts in other philosophical systems to formulate their understandings of God. It is a need that percolates down to our time as well, as people seek certainty about the supreme being to whom they have devoted themselves.

The iconoclast tendency in early Christian theology disturbed at least one desert Christian's innocent faith, and the fact that his story was recorded speaks well of the desert Christian community. Perhaps this man was not alone in savoring his use of imagination to imagine God in a form that worked affectively in his prayer life. The story goes that this Christian, who was named Serapion and was a desert dweller for fifty or more years, was convinced through argument that his tendency to anthropomorphize God was an error. Logically, he could assent to the biblical exegesis his friends offered. Yet, experientially, his heart had not shifted; when they began to pray, he was distressed, not knowing where to turn his thoughts or what to hold onto. Notably, John Cassian includes in his account of this story the compassion of those who witnessed and shared Serapion's distress, which motivated them to ask another wise elder, Isaac, how to account for the persistence of this error.[15] Isaac charitably explains how this error is not the fruit of some new demonic temptation but rather an ancient error associated with ignorance. He likens Serapion's condition to that of other pagans who simply have not yet come to understand the truth about God's imagelessness. Cassian's work is certainly polemical, reflected on after his visiting so many desert Christians in the fourth century and using the opportunity to recall teachings from important elders to lead his readers through practical and theoretical matters.

For me, what is important in this story, as a representative text of early experimentation around ways God might be encountered, is the strictly anti-materialist bent of these thinkers. Instead of discerning God's ubiquity as being capable of being expressed both within an anthropomorphizing imagination and in other ways, these thinkers sought to reify and make universal one way in which God could and should be regarded. This bent occasions the much later critique, offered by Lynn White Jr., of Christianity's role in hastening climate change. If Christian theologians had been more comfortable taking their incarnational and sacramental theology seriously and valuing matter as sacred, we would certainly live in a different world today. Thinking of incarnation and sacramentality in new—though perhaps ancient—ways is an invitation for our time. Perhaps like Serapion and so-called pagans, we might consider the form of created beings sacred, worthy of veneration not because of their representing God but because of their inherent value in sourcing and sustaining the life we all share. While pantheism has been a theological position many seek to avoid, inquiring into the implications that render it suspect may be useful. It may be useful to consider how the power of some to negotiate access to the divine would be compromised if all were themselves considered part of the divine already.

The experience of theophany has been central to the formation of Christian spirituality. People's experience of divine encounter galvanized their identity and consciousness in a way that grew meaningful to others around them and even facilitated the creation of new faith traditions. Central to the experience of the sacred revealed in particular places is the expression of sacred being within the aspect of world revealed through such an encounter; sites and species are thus both divinized by virtue of association with gods/goddesses encountered through their material media and give rise to such associations. Mount Rainer figured as a kind of God for the Seattle-based poet Denise Levertov. Not that she divinized the landscape problematically, as a Catholic convert; Levertov read her own daily experience of mountain view sometimes being clear and sometimes being obscured by clouds or fog as a significant way to understand how she sometimes experienced God's presence clearly and sometimes did not. Her faithful conviction that Mount Rainer was always present, whether or not she could see the mountain, sourced her conviction that God, too, was always present, whether or not God was felt or discerned. Levertov wrote numerous poems elaborating this kin relationship that she felt between the mountain's geophanic presence in the landscape and how she might encounter God.

This way that a poet reads their experience to express their understanding of the sacred is exemplary in the Christian spiritual tradition. Of course, we know the biblical psalmists and prophets used poetry for expressions of both praise and lament, both inspiration and condemnation. The psalms are shot through with a fragmented consciousness addressing itself (when, for instance, instructing the self to bless God, "Bless the Lord, my soul!"), addressing others in the human community, addressing others of the more-than-human community, and fundamentally addressing God. It seems inevitable that once recognition of the divine has occurred, one would want to address the divine and, moreover, to understand oneself as addressed by the divine. The recognition would go both ways. Our status in relation to the divine might be humble or exalted, somewhat in the way that our relationship with the natural world can humble and exalt us. There is, however, little recognition of us by means of ocean, forest, desert, or mountain. When in these places that evoke tremendous awe in ourselves and in our ancient forebears, we may simultaneously feel our aloneness and our belongingness. The paradox involved in these dual realizations may have something to do with identifying the divine other.

Where, one might ask, is not the divine? Could the divine by any reason of divine being not be somewhere? The pervasiveness of divine being is constitutive of divine being, so we can never get away from divinity. As Psalm 139 notes with either satisfaction or dismay (or both?), we can never leave divine presence. This curiosity of our human awareness leads us to the unmistakable conclusion that every being is saturated with divine being, that divinity is in the nature of all things, ourselves included. In important ways, this upends our past understandings of divinity as related to gods and goddesses and helps us evoke the sacred status of all being. There is no place where being is not. Thus, there is no place where divinity may not be present as coconstitutive of being itself. The ontological conundrum evoked by such thinking tends to make my head hurt, but as I look onto creation and marvel at the uniqueness of my being alive at this moment in this place, it helps to understand that a word—like *divinity*—could be used of all that we see, hear, and appreciate about the life that surrounds us and about all we feel and are capable of feeling within.

Theologians have often distinguished between the what and who of God: we are the *what* of what God is, not the *who*. This is a useful distinction I have heard from Orthodox theologians distinguishing between essence and energies. It helps me to think of energies abounding through the universe that are divine and god /goddess-like. The distinction embedded in this who versus what also evokes the immanent and transcendent. The pendulum swing of feminist philosophy and feminist ethics emphasizes the immanent to the exclusion of the transcendent. That is more akin to where I am these days, though I suspect it is not a wholly tenable position. There may be a both/and of immanence and transcendence that helps us recognize the value and significance of all that's here now while fostering hope for what remains (for now) intangible to our senses, though real in ways that matter most. This is "the jam" of the divine feminine engaged by Christena Cleveland through her pilgrimage to find a representation of God with whom she might identify.[16] If we were to also see the land imaging forth the sacred, our pilgrimage to other places would also keep us close to the places we inhabit every day.

The *real* is an important element in all this. Do we want God to be an abstract figure not sullied by material existence? Or do we want a God who can get grubby with us in the here and now of earthly being? Does it matter what we want? Sallie McFague already introduced a helpful framework for thinking of Earth as God's body, and this is a useful corrective to the thinking that defers value beyond Earth. We can certainly follow her suggestion as we engage all parts of creation as indicating God and as expressive of God. I hoped I've also expressed my desire in this chapter to move our thinking within the immanent frame to summon courage to regard creation as God's body, as McFague described decades ago. Further, we may also be courageous enough to admit that our species losses incurred today and throughout this coming century will impoverish our understanding of and relationship to God immeasurably. That somehow feels insufficient, however, to underscoring the importance of what is happening in our world today. We need to recognize in some fundamental way the divine character of what is here and not as it relates to something that is not here.

appear o lord
in a flock of birds
so that it takes me a long time
to pluck you from the crowd[17]

ECOSPIRITUAL KINSHIP PRACTICE: ICONS OF THE SACRED WILD

Creating an icon of the sacred wild can initiate and deepen your engagement with a specific area of study within the Christian spiritual tradition. In this exercise, you will want to identify a figure in your studies who means something to you. For instance, I love and work with the Christian desert tradition, and for this exercise, I might identify Antony of Egypt or Syncletica or Evagrius as subjects for an icon of the sacred wild. These people are already pretty wild in their depiction in the literature. They are usually of a kind of rough human experience, with ungroomed appearance and long hair, sometimes scarcely clothed to render their voluntary poverty and simplicity. This is true of many other iconic figures from the tradition, for whom it might not be too difficult to imagine as representing the sacred wild.

What is an icon? In Christian spiritual tradition, an icon is a venerated image that facilitates relationship with the transcendent through radically immanent means of wood, paints made of natural ingredients, and the form of a bygone saint. Recently, iconographer Angela Manno has created a series of *Sacred Icons of Endangered*

Species, repurposing the traditional icon to express the sacred lives of endangered animals and plants.[18] These images invite us to query our assumptions about the sacred and how anthropocentric our views are, affirming human beings as sole carriers and conveyers of the sacred or the transcendent—perhaps because God's incarnation was expressed within a human body. One of my favorite images in the series is of an orangutan mother and child, evoking the familiar composition of Madonna and Child imagery and reminding me of the sacred bond between parent and child across species, a bond threatened as our complicity in climate change creates various challenges for the viability of our own and other species' continuance. The recognition of creaturely continuity across species is an essential feature of kinship play and of the strategies offered in this book to rehabilitate our understandings of ourselves.

An icon of the sacred wild is an image that calls forth our creativity and imagination to express the natural dimensions of the icon's subject. With the example of Antony of Egypt, I work with an artistic rendering of Antony, my own or a traced outline or printed image. I gather materials from the outdoors, preferably ones that have reached a point in their lifecycle when their removal from the landscape will not harm them or others. I attach them to the image, creating a radiating halo not limited to the head of Antony but expressing around and within the figure entirely the natural world of which it was a part, when alive or even now, if still living. This exercise may evoke for you the living context within which your scholarship on this figure or their teachings or writings about them emerges.

This practice is indebted to a student whom I met in my first year of teaching. Michele was in my first Introduction to Christian Spirituality class, and as part of her work in the class, she created what I call an icon of the sacred wild Teresa of Ávila. We had read *Interior Castle* together that semester, and as the semester drew to a close, the students had been asked to render an artistic response to the text. Michele's icon began as a charcoal drawing of Teresa praying with her hands clasped before her. Around and within Teresa's habited form,

Michele placed dried leaves, flowers, and stalks she had gathered. Michele explained that the metaphors Teresa used of the garden to speak of sequences in prayer life inspired her to create this rewilded image of the saint. The image evokes for me so much that connects with other ancestors of the faith (human and other-than-human), images we might play with to deepen our engagement with and commitment to the work of healing and liberation that Christian spirituality studies may contribute to today's world.

CHAPTER FIVE

Kinship Loss

Chaos—Dark Nights—Emergence

Learn tropism toward the difficult.[1]

When we have begun to excavate our own identities and that of God or the sacred, we may begin to experience *chaos* in the form of losing the foundations of what we thought was the real. This experience need not lead to despair, depression, or anxiety but may be the catalyst for the emergence of new forms of self-organization. In the moments leading to recovered stability, though, it may be difficult to settle on what attitude we are to take to the emerging newness of our lives—this kind of renewal is always happening, not just when certain expectations or understandings are undermined. The basis of all life is impermanence, change, and creation within the chaos around and within us—what might be experienced as awkward leaning into what feels strange and unfamiliar and allowing it to become familiar to us. Acknowledging the impermanent, change-driven, and ongoingly creative qualities of life could be an important moment in the current histories of our individual lives, in our work as a guild of scholar-practitioners, and in our societies more broadly.

I don't want to put too sunny an outlook on loss experienced as chaos or to overlook its very real disturbing dimensions. This would be disingenuous of me, especially when I, like many, struggle when feeling overwhelmed and as if the fabrics of my own life are torn asunder chaotically. Nevertheless, there is some comfort in the small routines that hold fast in these times, such as the moments before sleep when I can feel gratitude move through my awareness for my warm bed and my home, despite everything else that I encountered in the day. The small predictability of having a bed to fall into at the end of any day, however grim, can be an important means of staying afloat when chaos looms. Nevertheless, chaos is an interesting label to put on some experiences and to leave off others, and it helps us identify where and when we feel out of control—not necessarily a bad thing.

My own experience with chaos draws from being raised in a religious family whose members believed in the notion of rapture. At any moment, it seemed, the world was poised to become utterly chaotic—especially for the "unsaved"—and so living on the edge of chaos and wondering if I was among the saved characterized my identity and worldview. During my adolescence, the expectation of imminent loss and ending transitioned within my new cognition of climate change and the looming ecoapocalypse that many said was (and is still) upon us. The thread of resultant fear running through my life colors my engagement with religious texts harbingering end times and environmental literature that routinely addresses animal extinctions (including, eventually, that of the human species) and other ends to biodiversity, to the beautiful places and people I've known. These fears are not necessarily of a future possibility but also constitute an intolerance of what can remain persistently changing, and thus ending, in my life on a more regular basis.

Why the fear? I know that many religious people whose outlook is colored by millenarianism regard this time with confidence that they will be among the elect and that God is on their side against evil. For this reason, death bodes well for their sustenance and even flourishing—their immortality, even. A new, transformed (immaterial?) Earth is promised and imminent; it will replace the one many of us are complicit in having damaged so far. I was a pretty scrupulous kid, inclined to let my fears compel me to respond to numerous altar calls just to make sure I was saved and could be among those elect who might confidently ride out imminent chaos. This was not the kind of anxiety I needed as a young person, and ecoanxiety is not the kind of experience young people today need to live within. There are, of course, ways to channel that anxiety and trauma to productive action that is responsive to the changes that cause those fears, but to be born into a world that readily facilitates them is something we might challenge and change.

Death is a part of life. Certainly, little deaths happen all the time: deaths to our egos, deaths of our consciousness as we fall asleep at night, even what some call the *petite mort* of sexual experience. In all these cases of considering death as a macrocosmic experience that our smaller in-life experiences anticipate and reflect, we can see a particular dynamic at work. This dynamic does not undermine the severity of discomfort that chaos associated with loss and death occasions but also connects with something else, unknown yet often desired. The death of our ego can occasion a psychological reintegration of our pride and humility, our sleeping restores our bodily and psychic energies for a new day of activity, and even the loss of control and willingness to be vulnerable in sexual experience can lead to replenished intimacy with self and others. Because of this pattern that seems to enhance and even level distinctions, we will consider what feels negative about chaos, loss, and death while also keeping twinned within our consideration these parts of our experience that yield the goodness we desire.

THE CHAOS OF ANTICIPATORY GRIEF

Nature's resilience is phenomenal. As we grow more knowledgeable about the deep time within which our planet, galaxy, universe, and even what some consider the multiverses emerged and are emerging, we might cultivate a corresponding deep trust that what looks impossibly chaotic and amorphous will transform and is transforming. We can root our confidence in acknowledgment of our own partial perspective that, though essential to our own survival and helpful when combined with others' perspectives, changes over time so that what seemed one way once may not always seem that way—even chaos. A broader perspective may yield to patterns indecipherable at a smaller scale of time or space. Further, the partial quality of our own perspective hints at the need for collaboration in a way that undermines our individuality, autonomy, and self-sufficiency, traits that have, in many parts of our globalized world and colonized cultures, become our default modes of being.

The kind of chaos I describe being on the edge of during childhood and adolescence is a kind of anticipatory chaos, one that leaves the full thrust of the experience deferred but always flavoring the present. In allying this emotional tendency of religious life to what many experience in response to climate change, we might agree with forest ecologist Suzanne Simard, who states that irresponsible reforestation practices and insect infestations caused by global warming will lead to devastation for the forests in which she worked. Simard expresses regret that we have no word to describe this prescient knowledge and says that we need something to name the grief that attends this knowledge. "There should be a special word," she writes, "for the type of mourning you know is to come."[2] Why would such a special word be important? Isn't it enough just to feel and know we feel this dread? As with most language usage, having such words allows us to identify for ourselves what we actually experience while also sharing our understanding of the experience—if not the experience itself—with others. Creating new language, as we saw in an earlier chapter, helps us grow awareness together of what we are experiencing. Language may emerge from the experience itself, but many language theorists also claim that we do not have access to certain experiences until we have language for them. This seems to mean that people without a word for anticipatory grief may not be able to fully feel it or at least won't understand that this particular feeling is a component of their palette of emotions. The chaos within that is responsive to chaos without may churn restlessly without recognition until we allow ourselves to give chaos a name or allow ourselves to be named by the chaos.

I wonder if there is a way for us to move deeper into this seeming paradox: language emerges from experience and experience emerges from language. As an example, the artist and activist Katie Holten has devised a language of trees whereby each of the letters in the English alphabet is supplanted (pun intended!) by an artistic rendering of a tree, thus A = Apple, B = Beech, C = Cedar, etc. In her marvelous book, she collects writing about trees and pairs each writing with her own translation of text into the language of trees; the reader is presented with facing pages, one with text recognized as such and another with a variously ordered assemblage of trees.[3] In short quotes, the recognizable tree imagery standing in for each letter of the sentence is clearly discernible in orderly lines across the page. In more lengthy passages, the tree imagery becomes a veritable grove, so dense with leaves and pine needles that "reading" the text verges on the impossible. Yet Holten's task reveals our anthropocentric bias, our preference for considering the art as a stand-in for the English language rather than reading the messages through the assemblages of other living beings around us—of learning to discern and hear their words in their own languages. This, too, constitutes a newness in our sensibility, requiring loss and potential chaos when our own (preferred) modes of language use are destabilized. I admit to having Holten's book for several days and beginning to read several sections before I even could "see" the translation performed with every page (even the book's title and table of contents). It took time to realize that my own presuppositions about books and language were being queried and challenged by this artist's work. Holten's work is playful, and while it still ties individual tree imagery to an alphabetic script that English speakers may recognize, it nudges us beyond. Not only could we play with the crucifixion of our usual modes of discourse to herald the resurrection or rebirth of awareness and understanding of other modes, but we also might connect this expressiveness with the understanding achieved in the biblical account of the Pentecost in the Acts of the Apostles. All the assembled heard the apostles speak the kerygma, or proclamation of faith ("Jesus is Lord!") in their own tongue. What proclamation of faith, as fidelity to creation's chaotic and fertile reality, might we hear if we listened well! Pope Francis writes of God having joined us so closely together with the natural world that "we can feel the desertification of the soil almost as a physical ailment, and the extinction of species as a painful disfigurement."[4]

Loss of humanity is a special sort of anticipatory grief in which some of us sense that our species won't persist for too long if we don't radically change. Earth will be just fine without us. We will become a mere memory (whose memory?). Who will remain without us? What kind of species might our demise make possible and even inevitable? These kinds of questions ride the edge of grief and the seeming impossibility to really reckon with the real end to our humanity—a complex situation that seems to defy the possibility of our comprehending it, let alone our doing anything to prevent or hurry it along. Another kind of loss that is beginning to saturate our consciousness as a species is a sense of our loss as specialness as human—the special identifiers that we adopted to distinguish ourselves from other species and that Western humanists celebrated during the Renaissance. This loss is what I think many mean when they begin to talk about the posthuman. Not just that we are entering a period when our own viability as a species is under question but also that we are entering a new phase of our identity as a species that differs from the humans we have made ourselves. In some ways, that identity is transhuman, being transformed by all the other nonbiotic mechanisms we can manufacture to enhance our humanness and redress our vulnerabilities. Even eyeglasses, for instance, become an extension of ourselves so that our human identity with or without them makes a difference. Michael Pollan's investigation of the caffeinated self makes sense to me as I think about what my life is like with or without a beverage made from the beans of plants. This beverage has become so entwined with my own identity that, without it, my being would differ substantially. The posthuman means something different, in my mind, from combination with the manufactured. It's more a recovery of the animality of our lives, of the reweaving of our identity into the web of life from which we seem to have wanted to tear ourselves and set ourselves apart. For this transfiguration of our identity, we begin to understand and celebrate how *alike* we are with others with whom we share our planetary home, not how different we are.

Carl Phillip's writing in Katie Holten's book captures this beautifully. The poet writes:

> I know a man who, whenever he needs to write, or cry, or think—*really* think—goes to a willow in his local park and hides beneath its draped branches. He goes there so often, you could almost say he's become *part* of the willow; he seems a willow himself; he marks a place in my life where I stopped to rest, once, but I couldn't stay. Then there's another man, long ago now. His body a forest when seen from the air in a small plane, so that it's possible to get close enough to see where the oaks give way to poplar trees, or where, if you follow the pines far enough, they'll open out to a field across which you can see the ocean. I couldn't have found my way here without him.[5]

What I love about this writing is Phillip's modeling for us an ability to sense how we, and others, become part of the landscape, a rewilding of our identity that does not require much more than just reseeing what we are already doing as significant. We might not all have willow trees in nearby parks that would let us merge our identities with theirs, but we likely have other places equally significant to us. And if we don't, this is an opportune moment to form such relationships and to let our losses, potential and real, be countermanded by the supplement offered by the companionship of all that is not human. Further, I love Phillip's sense that proximity is not always necessary and, perhaps, we could add not always welcome. In the case of seeing from afar, we meet and benefit from one another, and this modeling of the landscape and our part in it helps us understand one another better.

In this sense, Mary Magdalene's experience at the empty tomb helps us consider the fecundity of chaos acknowledged as a kind of anticipatory grief. Mary's experience is of well-developed grief, colored by confusion, and this may closely resemble our own feelings today. We already know so much has been lost and is continuing to be lost that anticipating more may be about our own species' fate. But until that fate is certain, we are able to feel grief for all the losses we are making necessary by fulfilling our own needs without regard to the effects of doing so on others. Mary at the empty tomb had lost a friend in Jesus, who had begun the important work of reversing misogynistic patriarchy. Of course, he had to be killed. Everything he taught and lived went counter to the prevailing norms within his political and religious contexts. Today, those speaking out against corruption, injustice, and the steep environmental costs of "business as usual" are similarly targeted, silenced, and even killed. In the throes of confusion over this state of affairs, we need to hear the call of what we can't yet recognize as the sacred—of some insufficient stand-in, like how Mary regarded Jesus as the gardener, an ordinary man going about his work. Significantly, this work is about creation care, of tending the plants that feed us and support our lives through absorption of carbon dioxide and release of oxygen we can breathe. When Jesus speaks Mary's name and she recognizes him, I picture the internal turmoil of Mary's condition as crystalizing around hearing her name. Her identity is pronounced in the recognition of the unknown—in a way that allows her to recognize him. The reciprocity of this experience reveals itself as fundamental within our own experience as we sense that whatever remains chaotic, confusing, or unreal to us now may announce a calling to us, affirming our own identities and vocations.

ECOSPIRITUAL LAMENT AND ECOAPOCALYPSE

The Hebrew Scriptures have as their underlying reason for being the desire to make sense of loss of land. The Israelite writers and editors of the text understood themselves to have been promised land and descendants, to have lived in a place wonderful to their purposes of growing into a veritable people of God, and then to have had that land taken away from them. Postcolonial studies point out the entitlement in the story and the way that subsequent readers of the text have legitimized their own occupation of land they believed available to them. The destruction of Jerusalem figures importantly as a small-scale example of the impact of foreign invaders on the land the Israelites understood themselves to own, and their psalms regularly express lament over the loss of Jerusalem.

While we might be cautious in our acceptance of the premise that the biblical lands were legitimately given to and owned by the Israelites, we can commiserate with the experience of losing connection with land—with the experience of people driven off their land by the Israelite occupation and with the Israelite people, who later experienced the same kind of colonization. Lament might, then, at times color our ways of making ourselves known to ourselves and others; grief at the collapse of the earth-based quality of our lives together in just a few short generations takes hold on our psycho-spiritual consciousness, with or without our explicit recognition. Biblical scholars point out that a feature of biblical lament is a pattern of calling out to God and demanding assistance. This kind of prayer may already be fairly typical of some Christians' response to climate change and social upheaval. It might seem to emphasize a rather passive style of response to devastation; however, many of the Israelites believed that God was responsible for their loss of land. That the Israelites called on God to change their situation models a kind of outcry legitimate in our own time. We might address those we understand to be responsible for our own loss of connection with land—through whatever means—and demand that there be a reversal of this situation. Again, passivity might be suggested, but it's a kind that involves the person witnessing injustice and requiring that change occur.

Most lament psalms end optimistically, expressing trust in God's goodness and justice and being full of conviction that the person lamenting will eventually be vindicated and experience the justice and even the other good things they are entitled to. The lament psalms' ending with hope also gives us a way of being in the world that joins an outcry against injustice that might shame the person who hears the lament and is responsible for the injustice into acting righteously. Perhaps a renewal of lament logic could help us move away from just the blaming of others that is typical of much activist and political discourse. Expressing a conviction about the other's empowered humanity to act justly might go a long way to rehabilitating relationships between those who have unjustly seized power and those who are subject to them through economic and other means. An ecological lament merely recontextualizes this work of expressing grief, outrage, and pleas for help in the contemporary moment and place, when much of our cultural devastation comes from lack of reverence and respect for our human others and more-than-human others.

Another practice emergent in our time is the erection of altars of extinction, combining the structure of ancient recognition of powerful sacred places with the need to mourn losses of species, animal and other. Constructing such altars entails an exercise in beauty and recognition that beauty and its creation as a task expressive of our species being could help us not only make sense of the current and imminent losses but also equip us to make different futures possible for imperiled creature kin. While these altars might be constructed as a kind of artist exhibition in a gallery or, more often, a public space calling attention and bearing witness to species extinctions, they might also function liturgically in transforming being and action in a kind of alchemical experience that hybridizes art and activism.

Similarly, the liturgical experiences of funerals for dead persons of creation—widely construed—enable the human community to mark the significance of losses we may otherwise overlook. For instance, just a few years ago, scientists in Oregon used the funeral as a means of calling attention to the dead (melted) glacier, having "died" not of natural causes per se but of anthropogenic climate change. Whether this liturgy was, in fact, cathartic for the human mourners left behind after this loss or a way to galvanize advocacy to address climate change is unclear. The coincidence of personal and social transformation suggested by this appropriation of religious paraphernalia also suggests a reactivation of what religion is supposed to be for and why it arose—as a human cultural product making sense of human relationships with land, our planetary home. These practices of lament, altars of extinction, and rites of passage that allow participants to acknowledge and mourn losses need to be supported, creatively engaged, and extended in ways that normalize the experience of anticipatory loss and anticipatory grief that is already part of our human consciousness and, if repressed, will only continue to do further damage if unacknowledged. Further, these practices provide a counterpoint to the celebrations we can anticipate having as well as our actions and self-understanding as creature kin to so many imperiled species, making them life-affirming and life-sustaining.

The *anticipatory* quality of our experience of knowing how close we are to having our worlds completely reinvented remains potent for me. Many of us know that we are not yet living in the way we need to in order to support our world's continuance, let alone its thriving. Living confined within a narrative of business as usual, we defer making sense of this and suppose that whatever small thing we are able to do is enough for now. The radical changes required of us might also spark our creativity and invigorate our living in a manner worthy of our human dignity. Lots of specifics could be named here in terms of the betrayals we continue to live with: the transportation systems we use, the clothing we wear, the food we eat, the homes we live in, and the employment by which we earn a living. All these, especially in so-called developed nations, cannot continue as they are if we desire a livable future. While many may not be ready to do without yet, in-between measures may not be enough. Supplying greener alternatives to what's readily available now merely reinforces our consumerist lifestyles and impinges on the qualities of life of other beings—our creature kin—just as disturbingly as our current consumer habits do. Coming up with more radical alternatives requires that we radically assess what we are and are not ready to change and to change them anyway. Hence, anticipatory grief for many of us also entails an emotional response about the dissolution of ways of life to which we may have felt entitled. I sense, though, there is more satisfaction on the other side of this grief than we can yet appreciate.

On the other hand, rather than just grief, there is a kind of anticipatory fidelity we might also live into that is described by Christian feminist liberation theologians, who affirm the need for us to live in ways "as if" we are creating the world we and others need. Trusting that such a world is coming into being through our actions, we commit to the kinds of actions conducive to such creation. It may seem a tautology to refer to our lives this way but we, in some deep sense, need to elaborate what anticipatory fidelity might look like. Some may consider these actions valueless in light of the growing needs, but anticipatory fidelity means we act as if our actions make a difference. We trust the process, not knowing how the outcome may come about but willing to do our small part. This allows us to balance the larger-scale actions that policymakers—and we, in electing them—might be responsible for and the smaller-scale actions within our reach.

These two anticipatory reactions to life in the present—of grief and of faith—may be essential to cultivate at this time. They could be, in a sense, the flip side of each other, our grief requiring that we find some faith that roots us to the lifeways we embody without numbing paralysis and our faith requiring that we be realistic about the damage we inflict on the world and create for and in our lives. Further, as we share these griefs and faiths with each other and stop deferring recognition of impending chaos to the future, we live with more integrity in the present. We also realize that for many members of the Earth community, human and more-than-human, the chaos of ecoapocalypse has already defined their lives. The privilege to reflect on the status of our fear and to cultivate faith means we still live far from the essential impacts experienced by many at this time of significant changes. Shaking loose our attachment to our privilege and sharing the lot of others in compassionate solidarity means deepening our anticipatory griefs and faiths until they can no longer preoccupy us, having become simply a part of our being.

I wonder if we can align some of our resistance to grieving with what has been named white fragility in racial injustice work as ecospiritual fragility. What would this look like? I imagine it emerges as resistance to wanting to know not just what our bad feelings about the state of the world are but also how we're connected with causing the current state of things. This quality emerged in my own recent discomfort when walking past a place where I had recently seen a squirrel dragging ki's legs behind ki as ki slowly climbed some paved stairs to a walkway through a front lawn.[6] I was perplexed by the squirrel's actions but considered that it was possible the animal had been hit by a car or been disabled in some other way that meant ki probably wouldn't survive long. If ki's back was already broken, ki wouldn't be able to get away if another animal came along to antagonize ki. I wished at the time that I had more resources available to know what to do if I could catch the squirrel and help ki survive longer. I had no such resources, and so my later discomfort in even being on the same block as this happening was about both my inadequacy and my recognition that my species and our activities were likely sources of this animal's condition. My discomfort was real, but I could sense another part of me wanting to name it ecospiritual fragility. This term refers to our inability or resistance to owning our complicity in the fracturing of our kinship relation with other members of the Earth community and our tolerance of feeling squeamish, disgusted, or otherwise repelled by confrontation with evidence of this complicity. Our owning of this susceptibility in our experience today and learning to live through it to developing ecospiritual maturity is a vital task for our work as scholars, teachers, and pastors of multiple forms of creature kin impacted by our species' immaturity.

Biblical imagery of worlds ending is repurposed today by climate scientists acknowledging the severe changes rippling out over various ecosystems due to global warming. The entangled nature of our planetary reality gives rise to uncertainty about the impending losses. While habitat loss forces animals and people to migrate over terrain to find new worlds to inhabit and animal species are dying due to changes in their abilities to procure food and to reproduce, rising tidal waters also threaten the viability of island homes for many. These changes occasion endings of worlds. One future ending doesn't make sense anymore; so many worlds are rapidly destabilizing and collapsing. Some may argue that biblical imagery of apocalypse is uncanny for this moment of time. Others may object that the imagery can foster complacency and an attitude of endless deferral to a future possible ending. Land loss, of course, was the central critical crisis of the Hebrew Scriptures, and though the entitlement to land expressed in the biblical stories may be questioned, the dislocation of the Israelites and their deep lamentation over this dislocation occasions recognition of how vital our connection with land remains. The Hebrew Bible is the product of a people's considering the living through the end of a world—a world that may have never been legitimately theirs to begin with, and this relates almost seamlessly to our world today.

As many of us grieve the endings of worlds we inhabit and contribute to, we have an opportunity to recognize that for others, our creating an unjust world through a military-industrial-capitalist culture has *been* occasioning endings of worlds for humans and other-than-humans for a long time. The physical and cultural genocide of Indigenous peoples in my own country, for instance, is a case where endings of worlds have continued to happen as massacres, relocation, reeducation, and the like were imposed on them and their ways of life. Happily, decolonization of cultural forms such as language and food have emerged within the twenty-first century to rehabilitate these losses, and it remains important to recognize the ongoing vitality of Indigenous peoples and ways of life, despite the forces garnered against them. Further, for some animal and plant species, extirpation and extinction are endings that we won't yet know how to grapple with. Whether and how some of these species are able to reemerge or whether we have to live with the finality of the losses of their uniqueness, we may not know. Desiring to know may be natural, but it may also spring from an absolutist mindset too readily associated with patriarchy and white supremacy. Deferring our own work to a future ecoapocalyptic reality expresses only disrespect for the reality of species losses that we remain indelibly complicit in. While we need to attend to the grief some feel at these losses, we also need to act and hold our acting in balance with responding to the agency of these creature kin.

THE ECOMYSTICAL ITINERARY

Anyone familiar with the work of Christian mystics knows that paradox is a fundamental aspect of the experience of God or the sacred, known and unknown. Imagery of seeming polarities like light and dark, speech and silence, and solitude and community help these mystics make sense of what they can understand about their experience of God or the sacred and what they have to inevitably let go of expecting to understand. The mystical itinerary has consisted of asceticism, illumination, and union. Typically, these stages map onto the aspects of body, mind, and spirit that constitute an individual as an indivisible being. To begin to see this itinerary in its ecospiritual iteration, we would map the experiences associated with each of them onto our contemporary experience of living amid significant ecological and cultural changes. Asceticism, as the first node on this ecospiritual itinerary, evokes the ways we bodily show up in the world and the intentional modifications we make as we learn to live more companionably with our creature kin. As discussed earlier in this book, green asceticism would be training ourselves to live in ways that effect less damage to the lifeways of our creature kin. Decisions about the food we eat, the dwellings we inhabit, the clothing we wear, and the ways we get from one place to another all would be factored into our experience of the ecomystical beginning.

Illumination as the ecomystical itinerary's second node would evoke the knowledge we gain when placing our bodies in communion with creature kin. What trickles into our minds from our body's knowing and this knowing in relation to the rest of the living world awakens a new part of us, one increasingly courageous enough to decide and be willing to do things that create a more abundant future for ourselves and our creature kin. Between this moment of illumination and union, however, usually emerges some unique challenge as we realize that our knowing will never be as full as we desire, that some crucial piece of the puzzle of our desired knowing will remain withheld. This has often been the place that occasions abuses of power, for when people are desperately at an impasse, acceptance of another's authority to move somewhere else along the path may come at any cost, even to one's integrity. The dark night of the soul is the name for some aspects of this experience, and Steven Chase has helpfully used imagery of "dark night" to speak of not just our experience but also the planet's experience, akin to a kind of deep crucifixion we might juxtapose between deep incarnation and deep resurrection.[7] This kind of language appropriates the tradition in a way, offering hope to Christians that something beyond our knowing is always at the edge of our experience and that God safely leads us to that place, always beyond the present. Truly, this can be deeply consoling and instill the kind of trust that facilitates action and not paralysis in light of the grievous changes afoot in the world today.

I am also curious about how we might rewild the dark night and deep crucifixion imagery to speak to a fundamental reality today that escapes our easy categorization within the tradition. Though many of our ancestors in faith experienced culture-wracking changes like plagues, wars, revolutions, and changes in both political and religious power, I wonder at what feels like unprecedented changes today and about the possibility that these familiar images—or familiar ways of using these images—may fall short of what we need. Could we instead play with them, helping them evoke something new in our awareness? Doing so would push us into a place of discomfort that nevertheless, because shared, helps us respond to and live with the reality of the suffering we are causing and either experiencing now or will experience soon.

Certainly, the power of dark night imagery is that it is drawn from the wild world we inhabit. Every night is dark to varying degrees, and a moonless night is perhaps the darkest, depending on where you are and how clear the starlight may be on such nights. This imagery is potent because however lost one is in such a night, daybreak will always come. The cyclical nature of the day, with its regular periods of light and dark, is deeply reassuring to the human psyche and soul. Similarly, the seasons evoke an inner rhythm—associating lack of growth with winter, newness with spring, full growth with summer, and harvest with autumn—that speaks to another way to marry the inner and outer world in particularly rich ways. Our own lives, as natural and wild as they are despite being lived primarily indoors and with more human-built devices than our companion kin in the outdoors have, do help us make sense of what we experience.

The dark night is traditionally seen as fomenting movement to divine union. If persisted with long enough, trustingly enough, we will finally see the dawn. Familiarity with this cycle and with other cycles drawn from the natural world, such as the seasons, helps us understand the changes in our spiritual maturity over time. Greening or rewilding divine union suggests what deep ecologists mean by the ecological self, when we are able to identify ourselves as not just the particular bodies and temporal existences we are. We are also able to see the wider and longer ranges of life that sustain us and that *are* us. I appreciate in this context the possibility of demystifying the rigors associated with "achieving" divine union as the destination of the ecomystical itinerary, as it helps us see how we already are so embodied within the web of life that nothing ultimately can disengage us. When we realize this already-always-present reality, we are merely mimicking and helping ourselves see more clearly what we do routinely about our relationship with God: assuming a separation that needs to be overcome through the work of asceticism and illumination.

The ethnobotanist Enrique Salmón helps me recontextualize the goal-oriented nature of the typical Christian spiritual/mystical itinerary. When we read of mystics' experiences of divine union, we often read of feelings of ecstasy and the sublime. Often such feelings seem most appropriately paired with how we think sexual union is experienced. There is something splendid and spectacular about this aspect of human experience that, in relating to the powers that be, renders us speechless or overwhelmed with speech so that nothing we say can make sense to the rationalizing mind. Salmón's observation about relationship with the natural world, based on his own Indigenous worldviews, is that we should grow more familiarity with the natural world rather than focus so much on what provokes awe, wonder, fascination, and the like.[8] We may seek these outsized, ecstatic experiences because they feel good and because they may be a part of our *desire* in knowing more and being more present to what and whom we share our world with. However, the kincentric ecology that Salmón describes fosters the recognition that we are kin and, as such, should grow our familiarity with one another through our presence. We, creature kin, may still surprise each other as our human kin do, but the everyday living together fosters *familiarity* that right now is quite far from most of our experience.

Reconsidering our path in life as one that deepens our rootedness to place and the belonging we share with others, we can reengage the moments of the ecomystical itinerary. We can also make choices that train us in being better family members, awakening to new knowledge about the worlds we share with others, and cherishing our family resemblances and differences with our various creature kin. We might use Salmón's framework for advancing a kincentric ecospirituality wherein we loosen the hold that the traditional Christian mystical itinerary has on our wounded imaginations, separated as they are from their forming by the natural world, and begin to learn to train all our actions to elaborate our kin relations. Centering these relationships leads to specific actions on behalf of our creature kin, especially those that call for responsibility, care, and wiser discernment about what needs in the human and more-than-human community must be tended to, why they must be tended to, and how we tended to them. This breaking open of our spiritual journeys' linearity to the deepening of bonds in the places where we now reside and work is the crucial task of this time, as is reimagining the possibilities for our lives when we invite kincentricism to inform our thinking and being. This invitation involves balancing wonder and familiarity.

In the film *Wisdom to Survive*, Bill McKibben expresses anticipatory solastalgia when he comments that the world will never be quite as beautiful as it is now, never quite as diverse and resplendent with creatures as it is now. He says that though this is occasion for rejoicing and enjoying the world as it is now, it is also knowledge that constitutes great sadness. We, the generation living in the early decades of the twenty-first century, know very well how much is being lost. Though our offspring and coming generations may grow gradually habituated to the impoverished biodiversity and the lack of beauty constituting their worlds, we are particularly aware—poignantly aware—of how much of the world's goodness is being lost. This ushers in a new psychospiritual reality with which we as spirituality scholar-practitioners must contend. It could be a reality that stymies our work, that paralyzes us, and that makes us question the validity of the work we do—I speak from personal experience! But it also could empower us to root into our work more deeply and to embrace, as some of our theologian colleagues do, the apophatic—the radical indeterminacy of our times (and of all times) and our contribution to the emergence of what is and what is becoming.

> My tree
> had a secret wound.
> Not lethal. And it was young.
> But one withered branch
> Hung down.[9]

ECOSPIRITUAL KINSHIP PRACTICE: ALTARS OF EXTINCTION

In a time of species extinctions, memorializing losses can take tangible form when we build on an aspect of religious practice: the construction of an altar. This is an artistic and activist practice created and taken up by various people in the past couple of decades to not only honor and grieve our losses of creature kin as Earth community members but also draw attention to the *fact* of these vanishing species. While a religious function of the altar is to provide a site for worship, sacrifice, and supplication, an altar of extinction creates a zone where deep reverence is experienced alongside an occasion for expressing deep grief. Many of us have seen roadside memorials at the site of car accidents where a death has occurred. This practice of constructing an altar of extinction is similar in helping us identify places in our lives where losses have occurred or are occurring and to create places where griefs can be held and expressed.

While most of us will not have specific relationships with extinct animals we might memorialize in the construction of an altar, most of us do have relationships with changing places, peoples, and other creature kin through the texts we study. The changing quality of these lives often entails losses of many kinds. Locate a site in your home or workplace where you can demarcate a place to house objects that call to mind and evoke your reverence and grief for some dimension of life that has been lost. While I invite you to think of material losses like specific creature kin, we know there are many ways that extinction and extirpation of our creature kin is occasioned by and connected to other forms of loss. For instance, our work may intersect with facilitating or recovering from epistemicides of past centuries, theorized by Ramón Grosfoguel as attempts to extinguish significant ways of knowing and directed toward Jewish and Muslim peoples, Indigenous peoples of the colonized Americas, enslaved peoples from Africa, and women condemned as witches.[10] Whose pictures might we feature on our altars of extinction? Whose words might we begin to weave into our acknowledgment of and lament over loss? What objects help us remember and grieve these losses, inspiring us to foster the resurgence of wisdom associated with these losses?

Much of our work allows us to participate in the rehabilitation of some of these devastating losses of our past and in the human activities that link our life and times with those who directly participated in the losses we commemorate. Our altars of extinction can help us become more explicit about this work of rehabilitation, as we move some things onto the altar to catalyze our reflection and our interactions with others and remove things that have, in effect, done their work. For some theorists of the Christian spiritual life, the inner oratory was an aspect of the heart where meeting and conversation with God occurred readily. Withdrawal to that "place" could align with physical relocations but might not in some cases. Access to one's own interior dwelling place then became a critical means to keep alive the possibility of realizing God's presence even amidst challenging exterior circumstances. Similarly, constructing an altar of extinction with tangible aspects of the material world activates an interior response, mirroring the two altars. Like the religious altar, this interior place may generate energy for new rituals of worship, sacrifice, and supplication—to God, to our life source, to the sacred. This exterior and interior space enables us to discern what we really want to participate in helping die, such as our own speciesism and other prevailing worldview that allow us to privilege our own lifeways over others' lifeways. Laying the symbols of these worldviews beside images or words evoking species extinctions helps us imagine and live into the flourishing that our work makes possible.

CHAPTER SIX

Kinship Love

Compassion—Belonging—Biophilia

What do you love too much to lose?[1]

Loss, chaos, and dark nights—by which I mean periods and places in our lives when we cannot see our way ahead—will never be wholly dispensed with. Nor would we necessarily want them to be. Many dimensions of our humanity might not have evolved without these particular experiences and our responses to them. At minimum, we need to acknowledge they are there and that they constitute some kind of trauma even if they also catalyze new growth. Acknowledging their effect on us may allow us to develop the capacity to deepen our gratitude for the support our social and ecological communities offer us for withstanding these times and persisting into ones that more obviously contribute to our flourishing. We may even then be able to offer ourselves to these uncertain moments to let what is possible form and emerge.

Early in the history of our own species, and indeed more generally of life on Earth, was the emergence of *desire*, characterized as an impulse that through sensual discernment in any number of phases results in a preference for one thing over another. Such preferences could include a particular source of food, a place where food is readily accessible, the selection of a mate, or the place where reproduction might be readily possible. That impulse carried out through time is for life to continue and constitutes the erotic pulse of the universe through the so-called heartstrings of myriad organisms and creatures throughout time. Religious traditions have refined this impulse embedded in our bodies to a conceptual attitude that still retains its affect in our bodies. Often, we have been taught to distrust this impulse, especially when it leads to behaviors contrary to faith commitments. The role of sexual abstinence, for instance, in some religious traditions helps shape a person's commitment and availability to a number of other eros-inspired projects requiring one's deepest passions and energies. Overregulation of our erotic impulse to promote one kind of activity over another emerges from a scarcity mentality, as if we believe and act from the belief that we have only so much love to go around. Reframing this assumption to consideration of the amplitude of compassion, solidarity, appreciation, and desire we can hold in our bodies, minds, and spirits might allow us to develop and access more reserves of strength and resilience for meeting today's challenges than we think possible and to align our work with others'.

As members of the Earth community, we can see ourselves as having a particular kind of love we feel and express for our other Earth community members. Those beings who prompt our deepest affections are often those with whom we live or with whom we have some kind of companionable relationship. They may also be beings whose beauty attracts us when we see them in the wild. We can think often of ourselves as the source of love. On the other hand, we also are the recipients of affectionate care. Indeed, if we had a good childhood we might have learned to presume on this receiving of affection and only gradually learned to return it and pass it on. Participating in the giving and receiving of affection is a part of our sacred belonging. Robin Wall Kimmerer reflects on her maternal love for her two daughters as a way of schooling her in naming what is love in the gifts the Earth offers her on a daily basis.[2] That this kind of thinking of Earth activity might be derogatively regarded as anthropomorphism helps us reconsider: What if our own human practices of love are learned through the auspices of Earth love? What if we are still quite novice-like in our ability to practice the kind of love we are shown every day by our creature kin and by Earth as our planetary source and home? That we regard many of these other species as lacking in skills we humans have in abundance should highlight our skewed values; learning love from these others constitutes an important dimension of a rewilded Christian ecospirituality oriented toward radical kinship. These kinship relations we have with others, who are so often in some ways *unlike* us, offer us love through their faithfulness to their own species contributions to the functioning and flourishing of the Earth community. Learning from this awakens our own love and our own actions on behalf of the common ground we share.

This chapter's epigraph comes from Kimmerer's reflection on what kind of ancestor she wants to be and where she discerns her love is most awakened to the vulnerability of loss. Kimmerer and Kathleen Dean Moore, an Oregon-based writer and environmental activist, have developed a workshop in which they share the metaphor of two rivers conjoining. In doing so, they allow the workshop participants to join the identification of the parts of the world they love too much to lose with ideas about what to do about it. This joining of passion with protection is a strong element of the human gifts we can apply to our world situation today. We have been loved. We have been protected, in our species infancy and adolescence especially. What will we do about giving back some semblance of gratitude as we live more fully into our species eldership? Even as we face our own species extinction, what might it mean to be mature enough in our love for live on Earth to assist in preserving current species and supporting future ones that are better at sustaining life than we are? Could this also prompt us to become better family members to the community of life on Earth? Do we, in fact, love ourselves well enough to do the work at not losing our place in the community of life on Earth?

As I consider my own response to what I love too much to lose, I readily consider the various animal species who have accompanied my life in such beautiful ways and whom I read about as a younger person. I desire that our human presence restore the trust of animal species betrayed by human cruelty and indifference, especially in human urban centers where wildlife persists in ways that are more commonly unnatural to their own natural lives. We could yet radically envision a kinship relation in our cities as making our cities places of refuge, sanctuary for human and more-than-human climate refugees. I desire living communities that are refuges and sanctuaries, not temporarily but permanently. And should I also need refuge someday, I might find it among a thriving, mutually supportive interspecies community. I desire that we think differently about our habitations and about the habitual ways that we oppress and cause the suffering of other creature kin. Could we rethink our dietary choices, the ways that animal and plant bodies are subject to our material needs? I desire that we celebrate the permeable boundaries between our indoors and outdoors, between our wild neighbors and our own habits of domesticity.

BIOPHILIA AND ECOSPIRITUAL AFFINITY

We all have some natural tendency to love life or feel biophilia, according to researchers of the impacts of social and cultural change on reducing the time children spend outdoors and diminishing their biophilia. An affinity to a particular place or for a particular critter may emerge early in our childhoods as we discover and express our entanglement with place and critter through play and adventure. Increasingly, the world seems to be presented as less safe for children developing this affinity on their own, so books and other forms of educational engagement can sometimes substitute for experiential, tangible contact with the outdoor world. Landscapes and creatures' lives communicated through books and other means can be transformative, and I admit my own attraction to desert is largely made possible through an immersion in texts about the desert rather than visceral engagement with my own body in desert places. My own biophilia for coastal landscapes and their denizens is riper in me than my love for other landscapes, as it draws from years of formation beside ocean and among redwoods and other critters who made their homes in those landscapes. I still feel a longing, however, for what is quite different from the coast, and I can live out that longing through pilgrimage to places stranger to me than those I knew in childhood. There is a kind of dance we make between loving the land that formed our bodies and loving other lands unknown to us but that formed our imaginations.

The Christian desert tradition is filled with stories of pilgrims, those trying to find their way to places that would uniquely enable their heartfelt connection with God. These pilgrims were also people traveling to visit and consult with those who had become more established in the desert wildernesses. The rambling of all these people through wild places must have occasioned some distress in the creature kin already living there. An ethic of staying put seems to emerge as antidote to all this restless looking for belonging, and it is significant that the way this "staying put" was expressed as a wisdom teaching drew from the wisdom of the natural world. For instance, Syncletica taught, "Just as the bird that gets up from her eggs makes them infertile and barren, so the faith of the [desert Christian] who moves from place to place becomes chilled and dead."[3] Similarly, the notion of transplanting a tree to another spot was used in the desert sayings to advocate for the rootedness and the slow and steady growth made possible by staying in place. Love for a place might emerge through familiarity and the sense of a belonging that grows when we persist in one place rather than growing dissatisfied or expressing our dissatisfaction by moving.

When Antony of Egypt found his inner mountain, a place slightly cultivated in providing him with dates to eat and where he also might plant a garden and eat from the land, Athanasius tells us that he fell in love with the place. Similarly, Jerome writes of the beloved habitation of his favored hermit, Paul.[4] Both Antony and Paul found desert wilderness places to live where there was solitude, some trees, arable land, and water. Love of place (topophilia) is something we, too, might be invited to as we come to the place that most invites our living with integrity and in balance between our own needs and the needs of those who share community with us. For too many of us, dislocation from beloved habitation is the norm. Lack of a job or adequate housing can drive us from our homelands and from our human community that supported our growth through childhood and adolescence. Going off to college, for those inclined that way, has also often meant a rite of passage in which we are expected to leave home and make our own way in the world. For some, this can constitute a trauma, quite out of keeping with the educational benefits posed as the offset for the dislocation. Sacrifices of some kind are likely inevitable for those who stay in their home communities. I wonder, though, whether sacrifices are felt only when they refer to things our consumer culture has taught us to expect for ourselves.

Some of us may have found leaving home or a homeplace a means of salvation. It's true that both Antony and Paul did. And lots of other pilgrims in our traditions model desire for a place beyond home that might become home, temporarily or permanently. Perhaps some of us today live in war zones, literal or figurative. Perhaps our beloved habitations have been negatively impacted by climate change. Living in a world that creates occasions for *having to leave* a beloved place should give us pause as we consider how we might change these conditions. I wonder if a broader contemplative culture emergent throughout our human communities at this time might prepare us for contentment in our homelands and for staying put when we're able to, whatever the resources for working in, living in, and contributing to the good of the community. The dislocation so common to most of us today in so-called developed countries is a central factor in our cultural and spiritual malaise. So much of who we are we receive from the Earth community members who are indigenous to the place where we were born and raised. The alienation from this place I'm lamenting constitutes an original trauma.[5]

For those of us who are, like Antony, desert lovers, it won't be too hard to understand why Antony fell in love with the place in the desert. Even those who most yearn for a solitary place in the woods to live may identify with his making his home in a snug little corner of the desert with a mountain and all he needed to survive. We all were formed by particular landscapes and the presence of particular creature kin who made their home with us there, whether it was an ocean, forests, mountains, plains, rivers, deserts, or other terrain forming our main habitat. Yet I sense we need to continually grapple with the exigencies of contemporary experience that render connecting with our birthplaces difficult and even impossible. The places our heart gravitate to, but which our bodies have not been formed by, constitute an ongoing ecospiritual affinity with place that we negotiate throughout a lifetime. Our biophilic entanglement with the places we call home may or may not match what originally gave us life but can help us live more fully, more at home, in the places we adopt or are adopted by later in life. We thus can form close relationships in new places that potentially lead us to further venturing from home. The relative ease of global travel lends itself to ever further dispersals from places that call us home. Like many aspects of our human experience, this desire for and ability to travel can be beneficial and destructive. When we're able to vacation or spend time in special places remote from our homes, we are able to develop an ecospiritual dimension of ourselves unique to that place. We may be able to heal trauma or respond to something lacking in ourselves that is unsupported in the place we call home. But this tendency can also result in our taking our home landscapes for granted and not developing the acuity to see how special each place is. Especially for the many of us who live in cities, we need to develop an appreciation for and celebration of an urban ecospirituality and all the wildlife that persists in these places rather than use every opportunity to leave the city to visit special, green, coastal, mountainous areas elsewhere. The habits of our lives might be usefully revitalized when we sense the ordinariness of a life among interspecies relationships.

Developing ecospiritual affinity is not easy, as it is defined by spontaneity and as something we do not necessarily control. Either we feel a certain way about a place or we don't. And that's okay. We don't need to manufacture feelings for places other people tell us are beautiful or special while our own hearts yearn to be elsewhere. Instead, we need to attend to where something about our lives is telling us we're in the wrong place for whatever reason, and if it's possible for us to return to the places in which we feel most ourselves, to do so. There is where the deepest community bonding can happen, our deepest energies can be called upon to root in soil familiar to us, and our deepest pleasure at being alive and at work and play on behalf of the community that sustains us can be activated. This is also the place that feels most like kin, I think, and where we are most able to tolerate and address the woundedness of place, working on behalf of repair for this particular place out of our deep love and compassion for it.

Most of us work in adopted places, and like human adopted families, the kin created in those places may be as important to us as the places we have left behind.

Learning our own language of felt biophilia and ecospiritual affinity requires we attend to how we feel in the places that we are able to make home and how we feel about places known to us through others' stories and through our imaginations. A radical continuity of self-acceptance and acceptance of these places exists when we can loosen the hold modernity places on our imagination, which tells us the more beautiful, the better. Learning to discern the truth and character of the place we live within also requires that we form possibly difficult and persistent relationships with the peoples of our places, including those neighbors we prefer to ignore or—worse—have removed. Living companionably and accepting the consequences of life together can open us to surprising connections, just as relations to our human family members can when we persist with them through failure, disappointment, and shared trauma. Accepting that it may require courage to remain present with what appears at first ugly or degraded (I think of concrete, polluted rivers, clear-cut forests, etc.) is also a way of awakening our compassion for these places and for the creatures who have no choice but to persist in the vicinity of wounded landscapes.

EROTIC, AGAPIC, PHILAUTIC, AND STORGIC ECOLOGIES

The German biologist Andreas Weber reflects on the erotic dimensions of ecology in his *Matter and Desire*. His work helps us think about the physicality of how love manifests, rooted here in the matter of our own bodies and of the landscapes dear to us. Ecology is a discipline that focuses on relationships between living organisms and their environments. Therefore, it helps Christian spirituality scholar-practitioners tend the quality of relationships that comprise the experiences we study, those of our own lives and the lives of those who wrote about and pondered such relationships. Consideration of Earth and the more-than-human should never be far from our study of relationships, for they constitute not only our physical being but our spiritual as well, the two essentially bound up in one another.

Many biblical narratives focus on the longing of people to return to a land that was kin to them. It hadn't been their own land, of course, and that's an important thing for Christian readers of the Bible to remember. The use of some of these texts to pattern colonization in later centuries is hugely problematic, and many Indigenous readers of the Bible can identify not only with the Israelites—the Hebrew Scriptures' main protagonists, who moved from sovereignty over themselves to oppression and assimilation and exile—but also with those peoples whom the Israelites displaced. Learning to live together instead of capitalizing on each other's life and labor might constitute an important ecospiritual principle to make real the beloved community Isaiah can envision, as well as others. But I imagine the Israelites' longing for land that they had believed they were entitled to is something that those of us displaced from our own communities can feel as well. The lamentations of biblical prophets for being separated from the place of one's nativity ring throughout the centuries.

Remarkably, the prophet Jeremiah opens his lamentations with the image of the widowed city, Jerusalem, emblem of the people's land. Because other biblical prophets used the metaphor of marriage to consider the covenant made between God and the Israelites, it is tempting to assume that this is an early version of "God is dead" thinking, this being the way that a city might be regarded as widowed. Just as God had been the cuckolded husband and Israel the unfaithful wife, so here has the city been abandoned by her beloved. I believe the metaphor takes a turn here, though, in the impossibility of declaring God dead. Rather, it is the people who have been exiled who have made Jerusalem a widow. Their dislocation constitutes a terminal ending of the marriage established through place and people. Building on this insight from Jeremiah, we might consider what places are bereaved of us. What places have we widowed? What places desire to awaken our own desire for them?

When we consider the prevalence of bridal and marital imagery in the Christian spiritual tradition, we note that it often draws from the Song of Songs to foster drawing near enough to God (one's beloved) to experience union—the apotheosis of the mystical life. As we saw earlier, reconfiguring this as an ecomystical itinerary allows us to broaden the identification of those in relationship and those experiencing proximity and union. Nurturing love for place and a place's creatures can entail pain, akin to the kind of pain that might attend relationship with God. As the Song of Songs attests, there is a wound of love, and this wound can move us into radically disorienting experiences of what feels like absence and loss. Opening ourselves to love of place and thinking of the marital imagery in light of our covenanted responsibility to the place we love occasions a similar peril. The pain of seeing a place changed, of seeing certain creature kin such as animals and plants no longer thriving in that place, and of seeing forest fires and other aspects of climate change devastate a place may be understandably avoided.

The threefold category of those vulnerable in Israelite society were the widow, the orphan, and the stranger. These categories speak meaningfully today as we consider whom, beyond the human community, have we widowed, orphaned, or stranded as a stranger? What places, especially, may be characterized by being widowed, orphaned, or stranded as a stranger when we forget our covenanted and kin relations with such places and their more-than-human inhabitants? Who among this larger community awaits our resurrection, our accompaniment, and our care? Whom do we love too much to lose but let be widowed, orphaned, or strangered by our lack of consideration and care?

While contemporary ecophilosophers may focus on eros as a dimension of our evolutionary drive equipping us to become the species we are, a desire we share with other creature kin on their own journeys of surviving and thriving, Christian ecospirituality includes various dimensions of love beyond the erotic. Drawn from some biblical writings that were shaped by Greek language and thought, the Christian tradition espouses love as *eros, agape, philautia*, and *storge*. Each of these comprise a nuanced sense of how compassion might be expressed and to whom it might be directed. Since eros is generally passionate, it is often felt as the strongest of these emotions and the one we express toward a romantic partner. Agapic love is unconditional and often associated not only with God's love for humanity (and all creation) but also with the kind of love we might incarnate in our attempts to imitate Christ. In Anders Nygren's exposition, agape love has several more dimensions: not only spontaneous and unmotivated, agape love is also indifferent to value, creative, and the initiator of relationship with God.[6] While there are many other things about Nygren's approach to delineating loves that I might not agree with, these designations for agape and the characterization he offers that differentiates agape from eros is helpful. For one thing, it helps us identify agape as something not just felt and expressed by God and humans but also pervasive throughout creation. Another form of philautia refers to the way we regard ourselves. And finally, storgic love is nurturing love when we care for others, as family members might.

Companionable presence may be one way we express our familial affection for creature kin. The Christian desert tradition tells of a man named Agathon who lived in a desert cave where there was also a large serpent. One day, the serpent decided to leave the cave, but Agathon said if the serpent left, he would leave too. So, the serpent stayed—a remarkable instance of the sayings collections reflecting an animal's agency! The story goes on:

> Now there was a sycamore-fig in that desert. It was their custom to eat together. Abba Agathon marked a line in the sycamore and divided the tree with the serpent: the serpent would eat the fruit from one side of the sycamore while the elder ate from the other. When they had finished eating, they went back into the cave, both of them together.[7]

While the theme of harmonious interspecies relations in the Christian desert tradition may be nostalgic, symbolic, or otherwise easily dismissed, in this case I consider the concrete proposal of life together described in this story of exemplars to speak to our situation today. We need to learn to literally live and eat together, even with creature kin who we would rather be elsewhere, who are inconvenient, or with whom we see ourselves as competing for resources. The possibilities for reconsidering our species commitments to our own goods open up when we take a story like this as a paradigmatic statement of what holy human and animal life might look like. This life would involve reconfiguring our assumptions over who belongs where we rewild our domestic homesteads and making companionable worlds for our shared creature kin. That Agathon was willing to leave the cave if the serpent left indicates to me a kind of longing for companionship that may feel foreign to many of us today because we bury this longing with other habits designed to deny the feeling. Agathon's declaration to the serpent may seem manipulative, but I hear a poignant longing in Agathon's words that speaks to my own longing to live in greater harmony with creature kin.

A storgic ecology also notes that animal kin care for each other, and some desert Christian stories might offer us ways to celebrate interspecies relationships and set limits on the negative interactions possible between threatened members of our creature kin. For instance, a story about the desert Christian Antony tells that he was walking when he encountered a family of birds and heard the mother bird instruct her offspring to throw stones at him so that he would not catch any of the birds.[8] A first observation of this story probably just results in our being astonished that Antony was able to interpret the communication between bird family members and that he translates this message into human words for his listeners. There are other stories of the Christian desert tradition that contain talking animals, understood by their human companions. A second observation of this story is that Antony, as exemplar, does not take offense at overhearing these instructions. He seems content to accede that he is indeed trespassing on the birds' home territory and that it is fitting that they desire him to leave. However, rather than retaliate or insist on his human rights to do his own will, Antony uses the situation as a lesson for himself and his friends, quickly metaphorizing the bird's instructions. Just as the birds regarded him as threatening and seemed poised to throw stones at him, so Antony and his friends might identify their own threats among the tempting thoughts that come to them and similarly "throw stones" at such thoughts to prevent being caught by them. While it's not exactly clear what kind of stones/thoughts these might be, Antony considers the womb of the Virgin Mary to be the cornerstone—an interesting change from biblical identification of her son as the cornerstone (Matt 21:42; Acts 4:11; and Eph 2:20)—which might yield a means of defense for Antony and his friends. This somewhat strange story reminds us that the lifeways of our creature kin yield life lessons for us when made into metaphors and that relations between ourselves and our creature kin are not always harmonious. Rather, we are often considered a threat by others among the more-than-human. To revitalize ecological wisdom to live agreeably with our creature kin requires a change of heart and behaviors.

PROMISCUOUS AND POLYAMOROUS ECOSPIRITUALITIES

We need to imagine differently and consider how we might operate from a mindset of abundance, not scarcity. Wherever we are, we are capable of loving that place, much as Antony felt love for the desert mountainous place where he was able to put down roots and to live well past a hundred years doing so. Our own lives today brim with love and compassion so that we can "afford" to give love to many places, and most of us are quite comfortable with this reality, having likely traveled to and lived in up to a dozen or more significant places through childhood to the end of old age. Developing the capacity to love these various places promiscuously, to distribute our biophilia and ecospiritual affinity broadly, allows us to develop flexible and spontaneously affectionate relations with our creature kin of any place. This promiscuous and polyamorous ecospirituality that enables us to spread and share our compassion broadly challenges the expectation that a romance with one particular place (be that our home place or an imagined utopia) will solve all our problems. Living readily into this kind of relationship with place and a place's creature kin (human and more-than-human) may be a feature of our time that can help us quickly discern, adapt to, and respond to the particular needs of the place we currently inhabit and join others in forming and being formed by it. While this promiscuous love might be used to justify the travel most of us are accustomed to and the luxury of enjoying landscapes strange to us, I warn us against doing this. We need to reconfigure our sense of entitlement when it comes to forms of travel that are polluting and environmentally damaging in other ways, disruptive not only to our own biorhythms but to the lives of other creature kin as well. Allied with this environmentally damaging practice our own bodies are subject to is the economically perverse program of export and import when parts of our creature kin—whether their bodies or products—are exchanged across borders. We need to collaborate to undo this bizarre system, engaging the aspects of the community where we live rather than expecting goods that come from beyond our community to be available to us or expecting we may provide them to communities elsewhere. Sensitivity to ecojustice has to figure into this collaborative work.

The twenty-first century is a time when we as a species are experimenting with new combinations of human community—with what may feel like new family structures for some of us—and with making sense of the necessarily temporary quality of some of our relationships. The dynamism involved in all this may be helpful in training us to discern ways we are becoming easily attuned to others and their needs and to the ways that others can meet our needs as well. Whether the quick catch-and-release form of relationships today will be helpful in the future remains to be seen, but I imagine that there is something important about our ability to question the primacy of certain family configurations so that our notion of kinship becomes more radical. Can we make family, for instance, with the unhoused human beings in our neighborhood, still on the way to a place that will be more permanently home for them? Can we make family with other migrating kin, flying above or walking through our cities? Can we make home together and, however temporary, a refuge for these others while seeing that doing so is good work for us to be involved in?

The formation of intentional communities and ecovillages also allows communities to come back together after decades (centuries?) of alienating isolation in the family unit or faith community and to draw people even of quite diverse interests, occupations, abilities, and skills to life together. Many neighborhoods may even have this incipient quality of intentional community-building with residents sharing meals, loaning tools to each other, or providing childcare for each other—that is, contributing to the formation of new life within the particular topos. The opportunity, especially for those without children, to participate in this kind of life together is important.

Even further, however, is the notice we are cultivating of our biological environment, of the gardens that are possible to grow in our particular places, of the wildlife that shares our neighborhood by day and night, and even of the weather that shapes all life activities in our particular topos. Considering the entirety of the intentional community we share is an important component to realizing the profound flourishing we can make possible for all life that shares our topos. Compassionate solidarity with neighborhood members who are not flourishing is important spiritual work for even those of us who are used to being in our offices most of the day. Expressing care for such members who know our own vulnerabilities will at times render us the recipients of care as well. The wildly creative sharing economies that we already participate in and might cultivate closer affinity to are a vital aspect of our ecospiritual becoming at this time: the use of library, public transportation, community gardens, public access to forest wildlife, and so on all bring joy!

To experience compassion means to experience with, not just to feel for. God's compassion for humanity invited a life expression to emerge from first-century Palestine, where divine teachings of love and forgiveness were communicated to a human following. This compassion for life cannot be species-specific; it is too profound for such constraint! We must imagine, even if we have no evidence for it since our access is to our species experience only, that some kind of revelation of what it takes to source and sustain life is offered to beings beyond our own species. While Christians tend to regard Jesus as revelatory of divine being, other iterations of this paradigm must persist throughout our biosphere and possibly beyond. We will need to develop better language in the future to communicate these intuitions and better interspecies communication may also confirm the ubiquity of the paradigm. The radical kinship that divine energies we name God so quickly knit us passionately together in a web of life in which God has fundamental expression. It could not be otherwise, or else it would not be. All would not be. Brother Lawrence's conviction that God could be experienced everywhere—in the cobbler's studio, kitchen, and community cloister—meant he understood and experienced the ubiquity of God. In one of his meditations, he pondered happening upon a bare tree in winter and expressed how his anticipating of spring reflected how he felt God's seeming absence to be the incipient declaration of God's presence. The natural energies and rhythms of biological life gave Brother Lawrence insight into how to understand his experience of God.

So many figures in the history of the Christian spiritual tradition have expressed desire to know where God may be located and experienced, even as they assent with their rational minds to God's ubiquity. The slim constraints of religious places were obvious spots to first consider God's presence. But over time, many began to look for and realize God's presence in other places, fundamentally within their own vital beings. That Brother Lawrence could regard, for instance, his inner life as an "oratory" within which God was active and might be prayed to whatever Brother Lawrence's physical environs were trains us to also realize and experience God's meeting us at whatever moment we are, wherever we are. That we may habitually regard our inner landscape where God dwells as a domestic and even human-built landscape is noteworthy, however. I wonder what happens when we allow that inner ecology to be rewilded, per Marc Bekoff's formulation—if we are able to open up corridors between our head and heart to let the thoughts and feelings freely migrate, just as exterior landscapes are rewilded to let our creature kin effect such similar migrations. The inner place where God's presence blooms was regarded by Teresa of Avila as an "interior castle." Building on her human-built environment of the city of Avila with its turreted walls, she reflected inward on the layers of space into which God's loving presence invited her to ultimately express the marital union for which the Song of Songs is celebrated. A loving union between God and God's people. The inner chapel. The inner castle. Even the desert Christian Syncletica spoke of an inner dwelling that had to be routinely cleaned to prepare a place for God, cleaning out all the hidden creatures that soil such a place. These human-built images for our interior life express quite naturally our preoccupying concerns with space.

If we spent more time outdoors and among other creatures, I wonder if other lifeways would suggest themselves to us as metaphor for our inner ecologies. The nest, for instance? Might our inner place of meeting divinity be a nest built of scraps of our inner worlds—the memories, longings, thoughts, emotions, and so on—in which a relationship with the divine is nourished and from which at some point our spirits take flight? Or might our inner mountain also be a good reflection of life outside our bodies? We have already considered the spiritual meadow as a fitting metaphor to consider the various wildness of flower foliage that a collection of stories might image. How else might we think of our scholarship and ecospiritual practice? Could they, too, be rewilded to image something quite different about the organization of our thoughts and experiences so that we become fundamentally content and no longer damage the world that so compassionately cares for us?

Not only might imagery of our fundamental natural setting suggest itself to us as we imagine our inner ecologies, but we might also consider our activities in our natural places as schooling us in how to think of the activities of our inner lives. Antony showed us a version of this when looking at how his interaction with a family of birds directed his thoughts to his threats, making a relationship between himself and how the birds viewed him with how he viewed his threatening thoughts. The work of weeding, of composting, of regenerating as applied to our work with our outer ecologies suggests how we might consider our inner work of scholarship and spiritual practice. How might we also weed out all that is dead in our inner lives so as to make room for what needs to be composted and to grow afresh? While agricultural practices might not suggest themselves as the most appropriate for rewilding, there is a sense in which the regenerative work of growing our physical food might also constitute something important about our growing the means of giving expression to our scholarship and practice.

As seeds are sown from our reading and observing of the natural world, we take the time to let them take root and to be replenished with the water and compost they need in order to blossom and fruit. The physicality of taking our nourishment from the natural world and the cyclical nature of this physical relationship requires that we make our scholarship and practice vital to nourish the needs of all the creature kin who live among and around us. They count on our being able to discern in what ways our work helps or hinders collective flourishing. This constitutes our deepest wisdom and joy—to figure this out, even if in the meantime it looks quite different from what we expected we might or should do and what others expect of us. Moving wildly into places of the mind and heart that are as yet unspoiled by human cultivation, we experiment anew in living with what is without attempting to despoil and change it—especially to reshape it into a place that more readily suits our cultivated tastes and inclinations.

I've struggled in this chapter between arguing for the rootedness of our being in particular landscapes and homes and among specific creature kin and allowing for the reality that many of us are quite distant from those places and those relationships. We may be able to identify this dislocation as a compelling factor in understanding ourselves as estranged individuals, communities, and even a species. However, we can also press past this binary to the reality that our lives are more fluid today than ever, with the movement and affiliations we form to and from within particular places. Advancing the notion that we can become promiscuous and polyamorous in our regard for varying places that claim our loyalty and affection may be part of the work of our time. Understanding how diversity also fosters resilience, living more fully into the particularities of our places and our identities means discovering newness and strangeness where formerly staleness and familiarity may have been experienced. We may also learn to detect how our healing, personal and collective, is entangled with the healing of places we feel for and that may feel something for us. Interpreting our feelings as ways that the place that formed us is feeling opens up our capacity to work for transformations inclusive of and beyond us. It also allows us to spread our love as widely as possible so that we can see that there is nothing we are willing to lose except what keeps us from perceiving the love Earth has for us.

If you want to become whole,
let yourself be partial.
If you want to become straight,
let yourself be crooked.
If you want to become full,
let yourself be empty.
If you want to be reborn,
let yourself die.
If you want to be given everything,
give everything up.[9]

ECOSPIRITUAL KINSHIP PRACTICE: GIFTS OF BEAUTY

In celebrating our relationships with creature kin, we need to accept the risk of realizing our shared woundedness. The same extractive mindsets and behaviors that have historically oppressed people are experienced by other parts of creation as well. This deep creaturely continuity that this book has elaborated makes the task of tending to our own well-being and the well-being of other parts of creation painful. All around us we see wounds, not just those that are metaphorically expressed within, in hearts and minds, but also in communities where the people experiencing homelessness are not cared for, where pavement occludes the thriving of wildlife, and where pollutants and disaster endanger lives. Francis Weller asks, "What if . . . the feelings we have when we pass through these zones of destruction are actually arising from the land itself?"[10] This is a wild thought! But one that invigorates my tolerance of feelings typically uncomfortable.

Trebbe Johnson suggests practices to discern and respond to a place's woundedness, cultivating alternative mindsets and behaviors through a deep respect for the trauma that a place and its inhabitants have suffered and for recognizing the place's resilience and implicit beauty. In this way, we build the capacity to release the energies too often spent maintaining the fiction that we do not live among wounds and trauma are not their source. Johnson's guidance for the annual Global Earth Exchange movement she founded within the Radical Joy for Hard Times framework are as follows:

1. Go to a wounded place.
2. Share your stories about what the place means to you.
3. Get to know the place as it is now.
4. Share what you discover.
5. Make a gift of beauty.[11]

Those who have taken these instructions seriously have found they can not only grapple with the difficulties involved in recognizing and responding to wounds, but they can also learn to see the ways that a wounded place is working out its own healing through resilience that we humans might learn from. For our own practices of making good on our grief, we, too, might consciously cultivate habits of tending to wounded places in our environs. When we note a wounded place in our cities, neighborhoods, or homes (even our own), we may share with others a story that demonstrates our connection with the place, realistically appraise the place's situation and our complicity as a species or even as an individual in it, and help foster some way that beauty may emerge from that place's woundedness.

If it's possible to tie this practice to our work as scholar-practitioners, even better. Could we identify a place that supports our work and discern that place's wounds? Could we share our story of knowing that place, seeing it change over time, accepting how it is now, and then offering the place a gift of beauty? One rainy day, on the sidewalk on my way to work, I encountered a small dying bird. At first, I thought the bird was simply stunned, and I knelt to keep the bird company while ki recovered. I held my umbrella over the two of us until I noticed the bird was dying. While I still hope ki may have been reserving ki's energies for flying away again after I left ki, to my inexperienced eye the bird was dead. I gently moved the bird's body to lie under a tree in the nearby elementary school's rain garden, leaving a couple of small stones and leaves to mark the presence of the sacred happening that was this bird's body. This offering of beauty was small, yet it did something inside of me that marks its changes in me still today. It was important for me to let my expression of awe at, sadness for, and love for this bird's transforming life energies require me to slow down, stay, and form a small natural assemblage to honor and practice the entanglement of our lives.

CHAPTER SEVEN

Kinship Vocation

Commitment—Ministry—Permaculture

> Vocation: calling, calling with, called by, calling as if the world mattered[1]

To return to Greta Thunberg's "How dare you?" mentioned in this book's introduction, it feels important to name this moment we are in as one *calling us* (from the Latin *vocare*) to various and new, even challenging, ways that we might be faithful to and contribute to the communities that have formed and are forming us. Significantly, we need to regard these calls to a vocational identity as coming not just from divine appointment, however we conceive of this, or even from our recognition of our human neighborhoods' needs. Rather, we must think of vocation as coming from all sides as we grow in our ability to discern and respond to the cries of our various Earth community members. These voices call us to commitment, to shedding ways of life we may feel entitled to but ultimately do not satisfy us, and to adventures and experiments in the way we interpret our activities—scholarly, pastoral, professional, and otherwise—as ecoministries. These voices also call us to consideration of how ecological design provides ways to organize our vocational lives, seamlessly weaving our work and world, indoor and outdoor personae, as community-based education and scholarship are emerging in the liberal arts in university settings. Certainly, all the practices in this book offer us ways to deepen our self-awareness and attunement to the world around us, to help us discern actions and ways of being that are conducive not only to our own health and happiness but also to that of others.

Ecospiritual director and cofounder of the Wild Church Network and Seminary of the Wild, Victoria Loorz theorizes that a *wild* ordination[2] locates us as beings ordained for particular ministries by the particular members, human and more-than-human, of the communities we share. This wild ordination constitutes a valid and critical framework within which to work, one independent of professional affiliation, educational training, credentials, expertise, or any means of earning a living that already makes up a larger component of our identity and labor than we might like. Playing with and querying institutional norms and theologies of apostolic succession, Loorz is broadening the call from the wild of ordination to indicate ways that the life of the whole cosmos has been leading to our own particular emergence and apprehension of place and purpose within the Earth community. This particular apprehension must not be definitive and fixed but supple and provisional, changing over time and open to the continuously changing and charged circumstances that comprise our lives and our relations with those of our neighbors, human and more-than-human. The suppleness of these calls requires that we rethink institutional affiliation, our credentials and accreditation, and the many other ways we regulate, monitor, and validate ourselves and others.

It may seem passé to regard the work of teaching spirituality as a spiritual practice itself, but I have come to delight in introducing and promoting contemplative pedagogy to educators beyond communities of faith and theology and religious studies classrooms as a way for many more to engage teaching and learning as contemplative practice. It may also seem passé to regard the work of scholarship as spiritual practice, to engage in one's writing and composing a life (Mary Catherine Bateson's term) as a means of healing oneself.[3]

But I have found this self-healing process a critical component in remaining committed to projects that seem either to evaporate into academic ether or to join such a slow-moving tide of thought that any meaningful redirection seems impossible. Certainly others, whose vocations emerge within pastoral settings and elsewhere, may also understand their responsiveness to the needs of human and more-than-human others as a key piece of their emerging and ever-changing vocation. They may also sometimes feel frustrated by the lack of evidence that anything is changing in the lives of others, especially for the better.

In our world today, the work of teaching, writing, and pastoral care is vital, although underutilized by those who are suspicious about this work's association with abuses of power and even with the so-called ivory tower. Increasingly, as climate chaos intensifies, we are going to need people skilled at self-reflection, compassionate listening and dialogue, communal discernment, and organizing. We are going to need people who have come to terms with living with the reality of their own solastalgia, climate grief, losses, and anxieties while helping others learn to hold the fraught power of their own experiences of these new norms. We are going to need people who have developed capacities and competencies in contemplative and ecospiritual practices so that they see their own identities as emergent with their community members. To whom and to which communities we pledge ourselves and our energies will determine what kind of work opens for us and how its value is accrued. This work may look nothing like what we were trained for. It may look nothing like it did just a half-century ago. With rapidly changing times, ways of working as a scholar-practitioner are morphing as well. Considering what these ways of working might still look like in the near and far future allows us to anticipate the changes required of us and to participate in the work of changing the field of spirituality itself. Doing so includes changing the institutions and cultural contexts within which Christian spirituality has functioned and continues to function and the economic context that measures the value of the various jobs we perform. Remuneration for our work remains necessary in our current cultural contexts, yet it may come to be something we are willing to revise as we live into and create cultures based on sharing and gift economies.

DEADLIHOODS, METANOIA, AND ECOSPIRITUAL MINISTRIES

Educational activist Manish Jain has aligned the word *deadlihoods* to the jobs that so many of us have that contribute to not only civilizational "progress" as modernity has construed it but also our own deadening alienation from ourselves, each other, and our Earth community. He does this in part in the context of spiritual practice, questioning the radical split many of us may feel between our religious obligations (going to church once a week, for instance) and our embeddedness within a capitalistic-militaristic industrial system, which we are required to maintain through our weekday labor and our debt. This dissociation is psychospiritually damaging for each of us, and it also results in negative impacts in our cultural and ecological settings. Unfortunately, too many of us might readily adopt this terminology of deadlihood to speak to our own malaise in jobs that have us performing and measuring success by standards that aren't our own and stifling our true passions—a parody of any notion of "livelihood" that would make sense of our work today. Making a living in this context becomes a travesty of how we actually have to spend our time. Jain asks four key questions to help us discern the "aliveliness" of our livelihoods:

1. Am I doing work that gives me joy and purpose?
2. Am I doing work that replenishes various forms of real wealth (such as health, social bonds, nature, local knowledge)?
3. Am I doing work that is changing the rules and policies to benefit communities rather than corporations?
4. Am I doing work that helps society go beyond an extractivist-military economy/culture/worldview?[4]

Being able to answer these questions helps us discern whether we are participating in the great turning described by Joanna Macy[5] and others or we have yet to lean into that vision. Similarly, Pope Francis has identified "ecological conversion" as a significant call for our times, both for those people of faith and people of good will who would contribute to a restoration of ecosystemic balances.[6] This call, significantly, comes from listening to what he names both the cries of Sister Earth and the cries of the poor (human and more-than-human).[7] That these calls are cries is also significant, because this is not a triumphal, grandiose announcement we listen for in discerning vocation; the calls that reach out to us now and that emerge from within our own being are those that resonate with the suffering of those we notice in our worlds and whose suffering we share. Joanna Macy's work aligns ecological conversion with her own questions that prompt active hope. They help us discern how we are contributing to holding actions that allow us to stop damage, creating structural alternatives to processes that are damaging, and fostering shifts in consciousness as we move from our current industrial growth society to a life-sustaining society. These questions are, along with Manish Jain's, useful to help us discern our own vocational directions: What are you turning away from? What are you turning toward? Where and how are you turning up?[8]

A great turning and ecological conversion describe the needed *metanoia*, or turning about, that we need right now, and it is a turning about occasioned by our revitalized kinship relations with the more-than-human who call us to account and to collaboration. Discerning anew our creaturely continuity with all that is assists us with living into new variations of old jobs and creating new livelihoods to support our communities. Already we are seeing a massive shift in possibilities as technology changes, meaning those online platforms that project job creations are naming new vocations coming into being; significantly, I have seen "rewilder" in one of these recent reports.

Just as homogeneity in our food systems has resulted in evolutionary changes to our inner biome, being less diverse than what was true of our ancestors' biomes, so our everyday activities homogenize our skill and decrease the likelihood that we are drawing on all our species possibilities in acting. I think of this often in the context of my university life, where I have an office and classrooms where I do most of my work. In a revitalized campus of this kind, I imagine more diversity to the way I spend my time at work and the activities I do. I would be spending some time with the grounds crew, helping care for the campus plant life. I would be spending some time crafting, cleaning, or helping with food preparation. The specialization required of us these past hundred years has been good for business, more efficient in producing a profit but less conducive to creating the kinds of lives that would be ultimately more pleasurable and satisfying for us, even if we do some things less skillfully than others. The ability to dynamically move through one's days, weeks, months, and years responsive to one's own body's abilities and develop a match between one's own dynamic growth and our communities' needs is a profound cultural metanoia we should create space for.

Some biblical call narratives have a pattern, discernible perhaps most legibly in Moses's call to lead the Israelites out of slavery in Egypt. This pattern begins with a theophany (or a geophany, as described earlier in this book) as a manifestation of the divine through nature or as nature manifesting its sacredness through a particular element with which we commune. In Moses's case, this element is a burning bush. Identity and instruction emerged from the bush, leading Moses to help in the liberating of the people of Israel. The first piece of the pattern is sacred manifestation, and the second piece is the giving of a task. In the third piece, Moses is not too sure of himself. He equivocates, citing numerous reasons why he likely isn't the best person to take up this divinely appointed task. Finally, the message from the burning bush reassures Moses of companionship and assistance. What this story tells me underscores much of what we have already touched on in this book: the curiosity that Moses had to pause his work tending animals to consider the burning bush that did not get consumed and to draw near enough to the bush to be confronted and given a task. The geophany as a manifestation through the burning bush prefigures all the ways we need to continue to watch for and listen to the sacredness of creation. Here, however, the particular emphasis is on Moses's recognition, through the playing out of his curiosity and the conversation with the burning bush, of his calling in life, his vocation, the ministry of liberation to which his—even inept—skills would be put.

We all have such calls on our life. The most important dimension of this particular story for our time is to invite us to attend to the ways the natural world calls to us as well. Burning bushes easily map onto forest fires, for instance, though we mustn't romanticize here, and the forest fires of my own region in the world certainly are consumed by flames, unlike the burning bush of Moses's story. But other such dimensions of the fragile, resilient world call to us and task us as well: the bleaching coral reefs, the broadening deserts, and the mountains corroded with mining practices. Each aspect of the damaged world about us calls to us and not necessarily to redress its own situation. Recall the burning bush directing Moses back to his own community—his own human community—to effect their liberation from a corrupt and harsh ruler. In our own time as well, we might consider the calls to return us to our own species identity and to liberate us from the particular cruelties attendant upon our human behaviors, like consumerism. Moses's call indeed emerged from memories suppressed deep within his consciousness. God's appointment was not news to Moses. He was aware of the Israelites' situation of servitude in Egypt. He had personal visceral memories of having tried and seemed to fail to intervene on behalf of an Israelites' plight in servitude. In this contemplative moment of encounter with the sacred wild, those memories emerged with a compulsive, irresistible pulse even as Moses simultaneously tried to draw on all his rational reasons to not respond to or be controlled by such memories.

I know we all have such memories as well. Memories we would rather not acknowledge for fear of the call they, too, might place on our lives, requiring our radical metanoia or turning aside from the path we thought we could see ourselves clearly advancing upon, all the way to the horizon. Pope Francis has advocated for ecological conversion as a dimension of our current human identity and activity.

He desires our becoming creatures being capable of change, willing to change, and actually accomplishing and committing to change. The hearing of a word and following of it usually precipitate this change. So many whispers of vulnerability still sound around us today from our human and more-than-human neighbors, offering almost more vocations than we could possibly handle in one lifetime.

What might it look like to consider our work as spirituality scholar-practitioners in light of a ministry of liberating our species kin for the sake of other species kin? What if we were liberated from the bonds of capitalism, anthropocentrism, sexism, racism, ethnocentrism, patriotism—all the kinds of things that require us to put more energy into maintaining divisions from one another and from our creature kin of the more-than-human variety—and put that energy toward loving and caring for one another? We are often told that we have all the technical resources we need and the financial means to apply these resources to redress serious systemic inequity worldwide. Yet there is no political will for the follow-through, as those in power put more energy into maintaining their positions than in doing the work, which might jeopardize their positions, of creating change. We need to act on our anticipatory faith in response to such strangleholds constricting change all around us. We need to let ourselves experiment and grow bolder in allowing ourselves to make mistakes while experimenting. The development of ecospiritual ministries means we *minister* to the needs of those emergent around us, understanding that such attention constitutes the most pleasurable and satisfying ways of spending our time that we could possibly imagine, even if it costs us in ways we can't fully imagine either.

STAYING WITH THE TROUBLE: TENTACULAR AND RHIZOMATIC ECOSPIRITUALITIES

Donna Haraway writes of staying with the trouble—that is, being willing to grapple with the complexities involved in thinking about or doing anything. This *staying with* requires being willing to part with one's commitment to something once new knowledge, new desire, and so on makes it untenable but being willing to stay when things heat up. This kind of staying evokes for me the monastic stability Benedictines are known for; Benedict critiqued the gyrovagues, who in his time were wandering about and taking advantage of the hospitality of various communities whose spiritual practice required they treat such visitors as Christ (RB 1.10). Today, I think of our own impulse to go off-planet as a kind of gyrovaguing, counter to the kind of sticking with it as things get difficult that Benedict and Haraway advocate for. This "staying with" needn't be an expression of miserable tenacity or "grim" determination but of compassion toward oneself and others as we forego interpreting such changes of direction as mistakes but rather lean into the difficulty of staying with what may be difficult and we may be even powerless to change. Commitment in a time of celebrating lack of commitment (e.g., the one-night stand; job and personnel turnovers; multitasking; what Pope Francis calls our throwaway culture; and other ways we enact our preference to disposability) is paradoxical, as even I am advocating a particular kind of commitment to uncertainty and difficulty here.

I want to trouble the association of ease and fluidity with what's discernible as one's gift, vocation, or ministry, because not everything that we're called to do is easy. This is especially the case when responding to such a call entails changes in one's thinking and being, not just one's acting. These changes can require a lot of work and even painful and exhausting work. I recall two examples of different mindsets about ease and difficulty that have stayed with me through the years, both representative of truths I have experienced and hold valid, though the two mindsets seem about as far apart from one another as possible. One mindset was expressed in the comment of a beloved piano teacher. Recognizing how long I practiced and how committed I was to becoming a more skilled piano player and knowing I would never be the exceptional pianist I wanted to be, they nevertheless encouraged me by saying that *it's only the difficult things that are worth doing.* Another mindset is expressed by a dear colleague who taught my students imagery of shoes to describe artistic vocation. Shoes that fit uncomfortably represent ways we try to fit ourselves into others' (or even our own) expectations of what art should and can look like and what an artist should or can look like. Comfortable shoes are better. And somehow shoes that seem *so* comfortable as to be slippers may be best of all and represent when we are doing our best work from our best selves. Perhaps we are surprised at getting recognition for doing things we would want to be doing anyway—not actions responsive to others' expectations of us but simply working from the sincerity of our hearts and the simplicity of our gifts.

Recently, this staying with the trouble amid vocation arose for me as a question of discerning how one's individual choices make (or don't make) a difference in light of the change of climate chaos. Andrew Boyd's *I Want a Better Catastrophe* grapples with the hopelessness that arises for many who are aware of the severity of our current ecological crises.[9] His book is a clarion call to the field of spirituality and ecospirituality, for scholar-practitioners to shape new practices, rituals, and attitudes for meeting what feels like an impossible, unprecedented situation emergent in our world today and anticipated to only get worse over the next century. Drawing on the traditions within which we have been trained and catalyzing them as resources to meet this moment may sometimes feel inadequate, but they may be all we've got. Discerning when and how to surrender them when they are no longer effectual for our time and place or to revitalize them to meet our needs constitutes a vital need.

Friends and students increasingly remind me of the value of challenging big corporations on their impact on global warming and pollution and of the value of advocacy and political action regarding policy changes that could affect big business. I hear this and believe in the value of recognizing this source of trouble in our modern world. I also believe that our individual actions support these industries and that tending to these actions themselves can curtail—pretty quickly—the motive driving these corporations' actions. The individual and the collective are totally implicated in how industry continues, and both our voting and our individual consumer choices matter. To argue for one or the other—the so-called bigger or smaller spheres of influence—remains in a dualistic mode symptomatic of patriarchal and white supremacy thinking. An invitation to both/and thinking helps us move more directly into supporting actions that make a difference for us, our communities, and all our creature kin.

Jesus's call to his friends is represented several times throughout the gospels with the simple words, "Follow me." His pilgrimage of ministries of caring for others through a short adult life did not cover much geographical ground but led to a kind of rootlessness that seems to go against the Benedictine stability mentioned earlier. Jesus is reported to have likened himself to, and distinguished himself from, his animal kin when saying, "Foxes have holes and birds of the air have nests, but the Son of Man has no place to lay his head" (Matt 8:20). I appreciate how this sense of himself expresses a kind of detachment from specific locations to allow Jesus the possibility of being present wherever he was, to be at home wherever he was. Theologically, this saying could help us ground Jesus's identity beyond the "human," as if he were reminding us that even within the human body he was not wholly at home, but deep incarnation expresses his playing through all the things and beings of creation. In another sense, distinguishing himself from animal kin effects a disruption with the belonging within the material world, which we need to activate and experience our full humanity, and flourishing here in a place that Genesis creation stories indicate was a home that was made for us and we were made for.

Similar to this response to Jesus's calling of his friends to follow him was the seeking that many pursued as they pondered Jesus's significance and marveled at all that was happening around him. Echoes of this admiration and quandary persisted into the first centuries of the Christian spiritual tradition, when revered gospel exemplars seem to have gone to the desert to experiment with their own paradoxical call to be present in a place and to a way of setting aside their own material advancement. In other words, they stopped contributing to Greco-Roman society in an observable way. Nevertheless, these people drew crowds of pilgrims who, like Jesus's followers, asked a simple question or made a simple demand to be given a "word" to live by. This word may be a fragment of a philosophical system to pledge one's life to, to mull over and to let take root in one's deepest being. The plea to be given such a word demonstrates such an utter, shared need among people to have purpose, to have guidance to the meaningful lives we all desire. In the face of what appears meaningless, this need becomes even more pressing. Today's "word" emerges, as I have claimed in this book, from within the human and more-than-human communities we belong to. These words invite us to stay with it, even when it isn't the word we would have chosen for ourselves.

In some stories from the Christian desert tradition, we hear of desert dwellers pondering the significance of seeking words of wisdom from others, of failure to put the words into practice, and of ambivalence in the changing relationship between those able to offer wisdom and those seeking wisdom. The desert dweller Felix was instead resolutely silent when pressed for a word of wisdom and then admitted that he had nothing to say, explaining that when there was nobody willing to act on the word that had been offered, God takes away the ability to offer any wisdom at all.[10] I wonder at a story like this and its sounding yet today with a kind of wisdom we might hear and act on. Could we consider our own times silent to us because we were not willing to act on what we heard? Could we even interpret Rachel Carson's story of "silent spring" to be a kind of silence that Felix describes, that of birdsong gone away because there was nobody to hear and act on the warnings implicit in natural responses to toxic means of "purifying" our landscapes? I imagine it takes some slowing down and commitment to stay with and hear the terrible silences of our world that are mounting now, as species experience a lack of understanding in our human hearing and thus forebear any further attempt at communication.

What is calling us? Who is calling us? Where might we discern a word? Where might we voice attention enough to express the quintessential plea of the Christian desert tradition: "Give me a word." How might we interpret a call as coming through the various experiences of care we want to offer and the love we have for specific members of the human community with whom we live and specific members of the Earth community whom we notice? How might our notice of these members also be a drawing forth from them that constitutes call? Just as the changing conditions of human family members necessitate certain changes in our own activities and commitments, so our attention to a broader collection of kin will bring new variations on vocation alive in us. Many of us know the radical reconfiguration of our identities, experiences, practices, sense of the sacred, loss, love, and even vocation that can be inaugurated by the failing health or job loss of a human family member. Called to a new version of the relationship we've formerly had, we cocreate new webs of reciprocal care and responsibility between us. Living into these vocational spaces, rather than resisting them, can constitute an important new dimension of human individual and communal life.

Early Christian monastic practice required that a person adhere to two fairly simple fundamentals: allegiance to one's human superior and to the human community's *rule*. In both cases, authority was located in the other and one's obedient response mediated through perceptive listening. Thus, Benedict's *Rule* can open with the important injunction to "Listen!" and go on to assure the monastic reader that the person's good was always in the superior's mind. We can easily see how this confidence might be misplaced and how those with authority could take advantage of a pliable monastic community member. Navigating the flux between authority residing within oneself (the postmodern dream) and within the other is part of our human task at this point. Additionally, discerning how various "others" might seem to constitute a separate authority yet reside fully in or through oneself is also a puzzling dimension of what contemporary deep ecologists would urge us to discover.

An invitation to commitment within Christian spirituality studies emerges early on in one's studies as various subjects offer a particular wisdom by which the scholar needs and even wants to grow. Narrowing these options to discern a subject for doctoral work, for instance, can be difficult and lead to identity crises: Am I a medievalist? Am I liturgist? Am I a theologian? We do not even have the kind of language yet to particularize our own work in Christian spirituality studies, often being called theologians perhaps despite ourselves. I have heard *spiritologist* used to name the spiritual studies scholar, but the term does not yet reflect what I think I do as a scholar-practitioner. Faculty members advised my own doctoral studies cohort to pick a dissertation subject capacious enough to dive deep within, not just for the length of one's dissertation research but also ostensibly for the rest of one's career and life. That was a tall order, for sure, and intimidating. What if one picked something that ended up not being capacious enough? When and how would one know? How does one measure capaciousness? Might capaciousness change over time?

Speaking for myself, I stayed committed to my love for the Christian desert tradition for a time, and I still believe in the capaciousness of the tradition's literature, even as my own scholarship has moved, at least temporarily, away from the tradition. Other currents have swept me in other directions. And this seems somehow appropriate for this time, even as it sometimes creates frustration for me when seeming to fragment the scholarly and collegial communities around me that might support and grow my work and with whose members I might collaborate and reciprocate. The hybrid nature of our work as spirituality scholars does seem to be emerging with this time, along with greater recognition of the pervasiveness of spirituality undergirding or embedded within multiple adjacent and even not-so-adjacent disciplines. We find our work to be perhaps too easily co-opted by those other fields, yet we likely need to resist the judgment that can emerge with that recognition—even as we defend the particular tasks of our field requiring training, practice, and experience.

Haraway writes of tentacularity as "life lived along lines—and such a wealth of lines—not at points, not in spheres."[11] I think of all the webs of our making, connecting us with various others and within which we live and change, and how they constitute our emergent contributions to what is currently needed. Certainly, one of the gifts of the desert Christian tradition is the concept of a desert Christian's idiorrhythmic practice, of moving along with and changing to the beat of their own heart's rhythms. When asked to pinpoint a particular valuable practice or way of life, for instance, one of the elder Christians responded with this open invitation: "Whatever you observe your soul wishing to do for God, do it—and watch over your heart."[12] This followed the elder's short exposition of the exemplars found in Scripture: Abraham, Elijah, and David, for instance, practiced hospitality, silence, and humility. God was with and valued each man's way of being. A certain diet, a certain mode of prayer, a certain sleep schedule, a certain amount of time kept in company with available others, a certain level of asceticism that made sense within a particular person's life circumstances—all this fell within an idiorrhythmic spirituality. Part of the quality of this idiorrhythmia was its modeling how, for us, a life's rhythm might change over time, and even the most complex accompaniments of rhythms might work in a way surprising and beneficial to us and others. This idiorrhythmia might not emerge linearly but circle back on itself, amplifying some dimensions of life experience at some sprawling distance while drawing back capacities along other tentacular lines. Such a quality of flexibility might be ours today and proactively embraced and embellished even as we query and move beyond certain expectations of ourselves in our performance of teaching, scholarship, and pastoral care ministries. Though applying principally to which ascetic and spiritual practices a person would adopt, idiorrhythmia might also today characterize a wider swath of our life's commitments, held in various levels of tension with what others around us need and what emerges naturally from our own life and needs.

We might, in particular, be more responsive in our vocational life expressions to the needs of the more-than-human and comport ourselves within vocations in ways sensitive to knowing those needs. To do this, we may need to start as beginners again, learning the identities and life paths of the creatures in our part of the world: What are their food sources, and how do they regenerate when wounded? What are their expressions of intelligence, communication, and reproduction? What are the signs of their suffering damage or flourishing? To begin to answer these questions, we need proximity to these life forms in ways that do not compromise their own well-being but that contribute to the reweaving of our lives together. In so doing, we grow in understanding and familiarity with beings who have likely been often neglected and trivialized when we centered our own spiritual growth and that of the (human) community members we have committed to. This vocational expansion will also lead to conversations with and deeper understanding of other human members of our academic and religious institutions and to transdisciplinary work capable of contributing to the renewal of our communities.

Further, the rhizome functions as a meaningful model for expanding our ecospiritual identities and commitments to foster resilient and flexible responses to the varying voices calling us to attention and to vocational ministries. Like the creatures capable of letting themselves be spread and secured by multiple webs of contact with other creatures and within living soil—rather than rooting themselves with a single taproot going long and deep into one place—our own human vocational being may transform. No longer defined by role, profession, or job, we learn various skills, applying them in various settings and diversifying our human capacities even as we let our ecospiritual lives take new shape under new demands. For me as a scholar-practitioner and teacher, this has meant desiring to be more active in imagining the possibilities for rewilding and permaculture on a university campus. I sense myself newly capable of hearing the land express desire to be more fully fecund for the various creatures, such as squirrels, rabbits, and deer, who make their homes here. I desire a professionalism transformed here, where I would be obliged through my responsiveness to the call of this land to work parts of my day in classrooms, in my office, or a more communal setting and parts outdoors, on and with the land.

PERMACULTURE PRINCIPLES FOR KINSHIP RELATIONS

I have been fascinated by the permaculture principles emerging as a way to practice regenerative agriculture within one's own backyard. The principles can be applied in various ways as we consider what is valuable about participating in a *culture of permanence* that is diverse, dynamic, and desirable. For instance, Vandana Shiva has done critical work linking dysfunctional agricultural practices of monocropping with colonizing worldviews, what she calls a monoculture of the mind wherein everyone has to agree and think like the prevailing, dominant—usually white, male, educated, wealthy, able-bodied—members of a culture. Ecopsychologists and ecotherapists have also begun to theorize ways that permaculture gardening practices illuminate the psychological healing that gardeners and others working in their yards, neighborhoods, and cities experience as they apply these principles interiorly and exteriorly.[13] Intrigued by this connecting of interior ecology with the exterior, I want these principles to be considered when we think about how we conduct our studies, teach, and characterize our numerous commitments as spiritual practice. For each permaculture principle drawn from David Holmgren's classic study,[14] I offer a brief reflection on its valence for us as scholar-practitioners of Christian spirituality and connect the principle with the radical kinship theme of this book.

Observe and interact. This first principle dismantles the already-crumbling assumption that as scholar-practitioners, we might have an objective, value-free view of our subject. Our lives are continually interlaced with our scholarship and various forms of work; indeed, we undergo the scholarship and work we do only insofar as it informs and constitutes our lives and as we sense it may inform and constitutes others' lives. We live it in the self-implicating aspects of our work, seeking wisdom for our own life journey even as we sense that the hermeneutical process of understanding and then applying our learning means we are not indifferent learners or students of our subject matter or of nature. The key to this principle is the give-and-take of subject–object relationships: as we observe, we interact and as we interact, we observe. We learn and experiment, allowing our understanding to change and the invitation our observations hold out to us to have new meaning as we move into changed signification of our work and changed self-understanding. That this experimental quality of the first principle helps us loosen attachment to any specific outcome is challenging but important, as it renders us aware and affirming of the dynamic quality of our work.

Catch and Store Energy. To do our work of scholarship and spiritual practice, of scholarship *as* spiritual practice, we need to know how to rest, to orient our lives, and to work to be open to the best means by which energies can flow through our lives and work. This permaculture principle addresses the ability of plants to store carbon and to be an extremely effective means of drawing down surplus carbon dioxide in the atmosphere. The energy exchanges that occur underground signal to us that much also happens in our inner life that we may not be aware of. Our rest, our letting energy suffuse our lives, equips us to return to work with clarity, focus, efficiency—although I don't want to overlook the significance of some work that seems inefficient or unfocused since we often don't know where such work is leading. Having tended, however, to our own bodies' abilities to store and mete out the energy we need as required, we continue to underscore the resonance between our own lifeways and those of our creature kin who, whether plant or not, have their own capacities for seeking and storing energy to source their own lifeways.

Obtain a yield. Not everything we do will seem to yield a product, and I think that's an appropriate gesture for our time, when much that we do gets quantified from all angles, analyzed as to whether it's profitable to invest our time in. This permaculture principle emerges from the need and opportunity to work with plants that will yield something for the good of the whole ecosystem of which the plant is a part. This is true of our own work as well, as we attend closer to the possibilities embedded in even what seems abject failure. Such a yield may, despite our intentions and abilities, contribute to something growing yet unimaginable, unknowable. Openness to this constitutes an important dimension of the work of spirituality scholar-practitioners.

Apply self-regulation and accept feedback. As we grow more aware of our roles in the systems of our families, friendship circles, and faith communities and in the ecosystem of our bioregion, we are able to self-regulate to the tune of committing no or less harm to others in our communities. Taking time to grow awareness of our emotional response to life in our immediate environs as well as the global situations we're complicit in causing, we grow capacity to interrupt old patterns and accept others' responses to us as meaningful signals to repivot. Though human responses may be the ones we're mostly trained to listen for, including those responses ready-made in the texts we study, we can also become practiced in listening for the feedback our creature kin of the animal, vegetal, mineral, and other variety offer us.

Use and value renewable resources and services. As we consider our work as scholar-practitioners, we have to think about how our bodies and minds function together to help us produce teaching and scholarship we can value. Many in our field and adjacent fields in higher education and pastoral ministry are commenting on the ubiquity of burnout and depletion of our energies during a time when so much is demanded of us. Furthermore, our institutional support—as schools or parishes—is diminishing; technological tools require our time and energy to discern how best to use them; and the significance of our work is in constant question given the gravity of the ecological situation we find ourselves in. To learn to foster practices that support our well-being and the renewability of our own energies is to counter the cultural norms that require overproduction, exhaustion, and the like.

Produce no waste. This principle reminds me of one of the principles of emergent strategy, defined by adrienne maree brown: "Never a failure. Always a lesson."[15] In attempting to live in a manner that cultivates our own emotional, physical, and spiritual resilience, we may appear at times to be wasting our time and energy doing little. We must reconsider this habit of mind and foster times for ourselves and for those in our communities to "waste," to reflect, and to create.

Design from pattern to details. This principle requires the observation and interaction of the first of these permaculture principles to discern something specific: patterns that exist in the natural world. Designing from these patterns rather than imposing our own and designing from the natural rather than the mechanistic means approaching problem-solving in different ways.

Integrate rather than segregate. Echoing Manish Jain's concern that we segregate our time deadeningly between what feeds or nourishes our souls and what doesn't (and typically our jobs fit the second category), here we are invited to consider what our work might look like if it were an opportunity to integrate more of our selves rather than segregate. Similarly, training for our work has likely favored analysis and critical thinking as components of our skillset, called upon routinely over development of other, vitally atrophied skillsets. To rehabilitate the integration of our selves and work rather than remain complicit in separating them, we learn to accept the messiness of this integration, the entanglement of what already *is* essentially integrated were we to let go of our resistance to this. Releasing the energies required to keep separate what folds naturally together will result in being able to apply those energies elsewhere, where more needed.

Use small and slow solutions. For many of us, this may be the hardest principle to consider, accept, and put into play. So many of us have been socialized to value the big and the fast. Especially in this time of climate chaos, we are likely to feel that the urgency of crisis requires an immediate application of problem-solving skills as quickly as possible and at as large a scale as possible. Yet much is shifting beyond our knowing already and the slow, steady, and small movements to which we contribute unwittingly are even making themselves felt. This principle requires that we trust and lean into various scales, temporal and spatial, that move beyond our sensing and control. If enough of us can make this move to trust, we may start to see more of the effect of such solutions and learn to trust them more. Certainly, a lot of wisdom traditions have advocated versions of this principle, and most expressions like this can evoke exasperation from those who are skeptical that these expressions foster overdue patience. I'm sympathetic to this interpretation of our wisdom traditions' pasts.

Use and value diversity. This principle affirms the crucial need for life to emerge and thrive in conditions that are not uniform. Certainly, it's helpful to consider that even the apostle Paul affirmed that not all of us needed to be the same member of the body; if all were an eye, for instance, where would hearing be (1 Cor 12)? Similarly, using and valuing diversity across the spectrum of our activities means we don't look for things to be or act the same but to express their individuality in ways unique to their embodiment, ability, and preferences. Even as there are some species markers we'll likely share with some other humans, there is an endless variety of things that, due to our particular history, render us either apt to do certain things or apt to do other things. This principle helps us live into the radically inclusive space that is not about offering a place and purpose to everyone but to radically call into question what we're being inclusive about. In Christian spirituality, this may mean willingness to look beyond our standard definitions of classic exemplars of holiness, to query our definitions of what constitutes a classic in the tradition, and to explore beyond the genres and prototypes we've been accustomed to regard as source material for our studies and learning.

Use edges and value the marginal. Bayo Akomolafe has theorized for "edges in the middle,"[16] which is a provocative phrase drawing our attention to a resettling of centeredness and marginality that can yet be reconfigured. As I consider this phrase and even the valuing of the marginal and use of edges advocated for in permaculture work, I think of the metaphors we have in Christian theology that are consistent with this unsettling. Paul's metaphor of the body politic still has a sense of hierarchy, though the revaluing of all parts of the body and indeed of the diversity of the body, is an important move forward and away from homogeneity—or what Vandana Shiva has critiqued as monocultures of the mind. I sense that the metaphor of yeast works even more potently in this transfiguring of our valuing the marginal. Small and seemingly insignificant in regard to the dough with which it interacts, yeast nevertheless works throughout a whole and constituting substantive chemical change. Yeast is alive, comprised of microorganisms that demonstrate the proverbial value of the smallness of the mustard seed grown to large proportions. Similarly, the smallness of our own being and acting today has ripple effects (another metaphor) in spreading out throughout the whole. Morphic fields—another potent image—are composed and tipping points are reached as each of us moves with faithfulness and integrity to our own discernment of the world's needs around us. Nothing among the options available to us should be considered too small, even as we grow in our understanding of the severity of climate change and the real possibility of human extinction in the next hundred years.

Another provocative image to supplement the marginal is that of cat's cradle, a string game that some have used to speculate and practice what nonlinear reality can look like. Having the string drawn from a particular configuration of fingers and another player taking the strings to form yet another design, this type of play models decentralization, a sense in which there is no marginal. All places at which the string is secured around a finger are essential for how the design is held together. Moving increasingly into our consciousness of being embedded within and forming a web of life with all other earthly creatures, we can celebrate our multiple layers of diversity and craft ever new meaningful representations of a life together and a shared abundant future.

Creatively use and respond to change. Andrew Boyd interviews Gopal Dayaneni, who proposes that we are going to need to grow our capacity to navigate the different challenges emerging for us now.[17] He characterizes some of these as shocks, slides, and shifts, explaining how we will need to become more facile in responding to and anticipating certain activities with no clear path to live with their aftereffects. All our work will in a sense be provisional and require a huge investment in faith. Though Boyd is actively pursuing grounds for hope in his work, faith somehow also emerges as a potent given. Even our solutions that are aimed at enhancing the well-being of all may surprise us with unintended side effects, precipitating shocks, slides, and shifts of various dimensions and kinds. Most of these will be beyond our control, even as we offer our energies to grow more nimble to minimize negative side effects, sliding then to new realities.

The clarity with which some ancestors in the faith received vocations to critical work may be something we envy in our own time, when everything can seem up for grabs. Alternatively, we can regard today's lack of clarity with new senses, knowing it offers a greater dimension of freedom than we might have imagined for ourselves, as we live past old definitions of what it means to be a teacher, scholar, pastor, or simply a human being. As we cocreate new realities and learn to foster therein the means to good creature kin relations, we are weaving anew a web of life that will continue to provide habitat for countless human and more-than-human family members in the future. How we do that and how we learn to negotiate conflicting values and needs are crucial conversations we'll continue to have throughout the century. The use of our scholarship and practice to foster environments in which these conversations can be had, including as many of our Earth community members as possible, is important work for us all to be engaged in.

The Christian desert tradition has a charming story of two men. One, in pursuit of the other, calls out that he was trying to catch up to the other only because God had told him to seek wisdom at this other person's side; the pursuant yells back that he is fleeing his pursuer also on account of what God told him.[18] How to reconcile these dueling claims to fidelity to a vocational call? The story resonates for me when I consider the following: the systemic realities we live within that require sacrifices of our true integrity and the real conflicts that can arise around and within us as we begin to register the manifold callings from the places around us, each able to demand different qualities of our attention and energies. How could it be both right to nurture our human species needs at the expense of our other species kin? How could the needs of our nonhuman species kin require us to give up things to which we've become entitled? When irresolution or incompatibility become defining elements of our life together, what do we do? Too often, we have allowed ourselves not to sense or fully feel these paradoxes. If we then have permitted them to be felt, we have often sought advice from those whom we regard as having authority and power to help us discern. Too often, responses have been shallow, seeming to be direct and clear when, in reality, there is no directness or clarity to be offered or experienced.

We must learn to live in the complexity of this time. We must learn to be willing to give up and transform all the ways we have become habituated to thinking of ourselves as capable and deserving, even in our earnest striving for what's right at this moment. This will constitute our species honor, integrity, satisfaction, and joy.

Whereas the world is a house on fire;
Whereas the nations are filled with shouting;
Whereas hope seems small, sometimes
  a single bird on a wire
  left by migration behind.

Whereas kindness is seldom in the news
  and peace an abstraction
  while war is real;

Whereas words are all I have;
Whereas my life is short;
Whereas I am afraid;
Whereas I am free—despite all
  fire and anger and fear;

Be it therefore resolved a song
  shall be my calling—a song
  not yet made shall be vocation
  and peaceful words the work
  of my remaining days.[19]

ECOSPIRITUAL KINSHIP PRACTICE: WHO'S YOUR FAMILY?

Genealogies usually take linear form. Biblical passages use language of endless *begats* to indicate successive generations, and it is important for many people to be able to trace their lineage to specific places and peoples. Curiously, we often use the tree as a life system to organize the relationships indicated by human family members. What would happen if we used the rhizome instead and tried to trace ongoing relationships that are not necessarily sequential or chronological but that are dynamic, nonlinear, and open to reconfigurations not only once or twice but continuously throughout your lifetime?

For this ecospiritual kinship practice, create as expansive a family rhizome for yourself as you can. Use material elements such as painted rocks or slips of paper that signify particular nodes of the family rhizome that makes up your being. If these elements can be interchanged and moved about—on an altar, perhaps—even better. Include your human siblings, offspring, parents, and special friends. Include animals who have been and are your companions. Include special trees or hiding places in your yard, at school, or in a park that you enjoyed as a child; include magical places you may have visited in your lifetime that are outside your hometown or country and that have left an impression on you. Include important texts, pieces of music, or films. Don't feel you have to site yourself as the hub of this network but rather build this family rhizome to remind yourself of all the interconnecting parts that have contributed to form you as who you are right now and that may—will!—shift and change over time. Though some members will feel stable, certain elements may move further away from an ostensible "center" while others crowd in as more immediately life-giving and life-sustaining in one time and place. Consider periodically shifting the organization radically to reorder your sensibilities about yourself and the constituents to whom you're faithful. Remember that moving the "edges into the middle" can be a powerfully profound movement to awaken new awareness of what is truly important to you and what you truly live and do well that others (and your internalized patriarchal self) may minimize too readily.

Regularly moving the pieces around and removing or adding some can become a meaningful practice, whether enacted daily, weekly, monthly, or seasonally. Whatever feels right for reidentifying—reclaiming and being claimed by—the kinship relationships that comprise your being and that make you whole. I envision a bit of the magician trickster plying their trade with a coin or marble hidden under a cup—moving the pieces as an optical illusion to keep you guessing where exactly the hidden object is. With each incorrect guess, we can imagine our own tendency to locate the self and vocation in one place as similarly mistaken. Rather, the web formed of relationships issues a multivalent call to action that is discerned differently at different times. Don't get caught up, however, with the web itself but rather with the reality it reflects and the way your actions are drawn from the web in which your own life is caught.

Consider, too, what beings have you in *their* kinship rhizome and include them. These could be mentors, teachers, students, spiritual directees, parishioners, etc. How do your responsibilities to these human others give shape to your vocational identity and activities? Having engaged the ideas of this book, you have a lot of ideas of what comprises kinship, of how fluid these relationships can feel, and of how to create and sustain belonging. The act of creating your own miniature version of the kinship relationships that manifest as *you* right now allows you to reflect with more intention on the kinds of kinship relations you enter into and contribute to, whether purposely or accidentally. Resist the impulse to curate a perfect rhizome of relations and instead document what feels real and authentic to you. Each tendril or tentacle communicates something and carries your life energies in multiple and perhaps surprising directions.

Epilogue

This book created opportunities for me to think through the grave implications of ignoring this moment in human history. This moment requires so much of us that we have yet to recognize or begin to give. Those beginning to sense the gravity can be exhausted by the implications in our bodies, our thinking, our relationships, and our vocations, as well as in every arena where we choose to show up and where we choose to hold back. It feels difficult to end this work with the conviction that all this will grow only worse, but it feels honest to do so. I also wonder, while stating this conviction, whether we might also learn differently, to hold our exhaustion in new ways. Then, at least, it will have been liberated from the task of keeping us from noticing and addressing the disconnection that so many of us can feel between the work expected of us and the lives we are trying to live. I sense that, depleted though they may feel from the overwhelming amount of evidence making it seem that our current lives have no meaning, our life's energies may actually be revitalized when directed to make transparent the grave predicament we are in as a global society.

These redirected energies will also, I believe, help us live with more integrity and ultimately, for that reason, with more satisfaction. Certainly, seeking our own satisfaction might seem an irrelevant thing to consider as species are extirpated and go extinct, as human communities flounder near polluted and toxic waters, and as our food sources are manipulated for profit. Recently, I watched *The Salt of the Earth* (2014) with my partner. This film traces the emergence of vocation of the social photographer, Sebastião Salgado.

I remembered with fondness that Fr. Kevin Burke, SJ, and Dr. Julia Prinz introduced me to Salgado's work nearly a decade ago, when I was a student in their theology and arts class at the Jesuit School of Theology in Berkeley, California. Salgado's dark night, encountering human violence and cruelty while documenting African migrants' experience of severe famine and war, incapacitated him for a time until he recognized that the way to healing was with reconnecting with his own Brazilian homelands, desiccated and wounded as they were by imbalances in rainfall, drought, and overgrazing. Salgado was inspired by his partner Lélia's suggestion that they reforest the vast farm where he had grown up—today, the place is called Instituto Terra, a model for rainforest restoration. As when I have watched similar films, like *The Biggest Little Farm*, or videos of the Green Belt movement's work, I was amazed at how rapidly the transformation of wounded land and human psyches can be effected.

Of course, Sebastião and Lélia were honest about reporting the losses they experienced in their first years as they began to learn how to do the work. I imagine that even as we start our own work, we, too, will experience setbacks, mistakes, and instances where we realize that precious time and resources have been wasted and that evoke guilt and regret. Yet I also sense the magic on the other side of our willingness to experiment and to be as careful and courteous as we can with what and whom we have to work. Who knows what may become possible as we do so? It requires only that we start. As poet Denise Levertov notes,

> We have only begun
> to imagine . . .
>
> how it might be
> to live as sibling with beast and flower,
> not as oppressors.[1]

May this remaking of our kinship relations be enough to catalyze transformations in human communities that benefit all species and all features of our precious home, planet Earth.

Notes

INTRODUCTION

1 Greta Thunberg, "How Dare You," transcript of speech delivered at the UN Climate Action Summit, New York, September 23, 2019, https://www.npr.org/2019/09/23/763452863/transcript-greta-thunbergs-speech-at-the-u-n-climate-action-summit.

2 Lynn White Jr., "The Historical Roots of our Ecologic Crisis," *Science* 155 (1967): 1203–07.

3 An important scholar of this work is Norman Habel. See his *An Inconvenient Text: Is a Green Reading of the Bible Possible?* (Adelaide: ATF Press, 2009).

4 Leah Penniman, "Exegesis," in *Black Earth Wisdom: Soulful Conversations with Black Environmentalists* (New York: Amistad, 2023), 253–58.

5 Lisa Dahill, "Into Local Waters: Rewilding the Study of Christian Spirituality," *Spiritus* 16, no. 2 (Fall 2016): 154–58.

6 Douglas E. Christie, *The Blue Sapphire of the Mind: Notes for a Contemplative Ecology* (New York: Oxford University Press, 2013).

7 See Janette Oke's Animal Friends series, with titles such as *Spunky's Diary*, *New Kid in Town*, and *The Prodigal Cat*, published by Bethany House in the early 1980s.

8 Donna Haraway, *Staying with the Trouble: Making Kin in the Chthulucene* (Durham, NC: Duke University Press, 2016), 102.

9 John O'Donohue, "To Learn from Animal Being," in *To Bless the Space Between Us: A Book of Blessings* (New York: Convergent Books, 2008), 74.

10 Consider, too, the phenomenon of "Future Library," a forest that's been planted and preserved in Norway for the express purpose of supplying materials for a series of books to be published in early 2100. See Katie Paterson, "Future Library," in *The Language of Trees: A Rewilding of Literature and Landscape*, ed. Katie Holten (Portland, OR: Tin House, 2023), 168–69.

CHAPTER 1

1 Val Plumwood, *The Eye of the Crocodile* (Canberra: Australian National University E Press, 2012), 15.

2 See, for instance, Eric Daryl Meyer, *Inner Animalities: Theology and the End of the Human* (New York: Fordham University Press, 2018).
3 See, for instance, Jeanine M. Canty, *Returning the Self to Nature: Undoing our Collective Narcissism and Healing our Planet* (Boulder, CO: Shambhala, 2022).
4 Ada María Isasi-Díaz, *Mujerista Theology: A Theology for the Twenty-First Century* (Maryknoll, NY: Orbis Books, 1996).
5 John Moschos, *The Spiritual Meadow*, trans. John Wortley (Kalamazoo, MI: Cistercian Publications, 1992), 3.
6 Athanasius, *The Life of Antony*, trans. Robert C. Gregg (New York: Paulist Press, 1980), 32. The idea of being a wise bee was a topos, or general theme of literature, of the Christian desert tradition and may draw on biblical precedent. I remember the late Sr. Mary Forman, OSB, sharing her research connecting insect life from psalm references with Benedictine literature. Memorably, she referenced Ps 22:6—"I am a worm and not a man"—for its spiritual valence with Benedictine humility. Similar associations between wisdom-seeking and other insects can be made. See, too, the endlessly fascinating book by Joanne Lauck, *The Voice of the Infinite in the Small: Re-envisioning the Insect-Human Connection* (Boston: Shambhala, 2002).
7 Moschos, *The Spiritual Meadow*, 3–4. Italics mine.
8 Thomas Berry, *The Christian Future and the Fate of Earth* (Maryknoll, NY: Orbis Books, 2009), 8–9.
9 Moschos, *The Spiritual Meadow*, 4.
10 Moschos, *The Spiritual Meadow*, 5.
11 Thomas Berry, *The Great Work: Our Way into the Future* (New York: Harmony/Bell Tower, 1999).
12 Thomas Berry, *The Dream of the Earth* (San Francisco: Sierra Club Books, 1990), 42.
13 Freya Mathews, "Burning Our Kin," in *Kinship: Belonging in a World of Relations*, ed. Gavin Van Horn, Robin Wall Kimmerer, and John Hausdoerffer, vol. 4, *Persons* (Libertyville, IL: Center for Humans and Nature Press, 2021), 100.
14 Mathews, "Burning Our Kin," 101.
15 Berry, *The Christian Future*, 117.
16 Berry, *The Christian Future*, 117.
17 Berry, *The Christian Future*, 118.
18 See Stacy Alaimo, *Bodily Natures: Science, Environment, and the Material Self* (Bloomington: Indiana University Press, 2010) and *Exposed: Environmental Politics and Pleasures in Posthuman Times* (Minneapolis: University of Minnesota Press, 2016).
19 Vanessa Machado de Oliveira, *Hospicing Modernity: Facing Humanity's Wrongs and the Implications for Social Activism* (Berkeley: North Atlantic Books, 2021), 60.

20 Octavio Paz, "Wind, Water, Stone," in *The Collected Poems of Octavio Paz, 1957–1987* (New York: New Directions, 1987), 505.
21 David Hinton, *Desert: Poems* (Boulder, CO: Shambhala, 2018), 8.

CHAPTER 2

1 Thomas Merton, *A Search for Solitude: Pursuing the Monk's True Life*, ed. Lawrence S. Cunningham (New York: HarperCollins, 1997), 214.
2 Sandra M. Schneiders, "The Study of Christian Spirituality: Contours and Dynamics of a Discipline," in *Minding the Spirit: The Study of Christian Spirituality*, ed. Elizabeth A. Dreyer and Mark S. Burrows (Baltimore: Johns Hopkins University Press, 2005), 6.
3 Eucherius of Lyon, "In Praise of the Desert," in *The Life of the Jura Fathers* (Kalamazoo, MI: Cistercian Publications, 1999), 210.
4 Richard Louv, *Last Child in the Woods: Saving Our Children from Nature-Deficit Order* (Chapel Hill, NC: Algonquin Books, 2005).
5 Richard Louv, *Vitamin N: The Essential Guide to a Nature-Rich Life* (Chapel Hill, NC: Algonquin Books, 2016).
6 Robert Pyle's phrase. See *The Thunder Tree: Lessons from an Urban Wildland* (Boston: Houghton Mifflin, 1993), 145. I benefited from Sallie McFague's discussion of this concept in her *Super, Natural Christians: How We Should Love Nature* (Minneapolis: Fortress Press, 1997), 118.
7 Edward O. Wilson, *Half Earth: Our Planet's Fight for Life* (New York: Liveright, 2016), 20.
8 First used by Michael V. McGinnis, "Myth, Nature, and the Bureaucratic Experience," *Environmental Ethics* 16, no. 4 (1994): 425–36. Cited and described by Richard Louv in *Our Wild Calling: How Connecting with Animals Can Transform Our Lives—and Save Theirs* (Chapel Hill, NC: Algonquin Books, 2019), 16–19, 21–22.
9 Hannah Arendt, *The Origins of Totalitarianism* (New York: Harvest, 1973), 478. Cited by George Lipsitz, "Foreword: Accompaniment as a Way of Life," in *Mutual Accompaniment and the Creation of the Commons* by Mary Watkins (New Haven, CT: Yale University Press, 2019), xiii.
10 Evagrius Ponticus, *The Praktikos*, trans. John Eudes Bamberger (Collegeville, MN: Cistercian Publications, 1972), 18–19.
11 "Psychic Corpus Dissonance," Bureau of Linguistical Reality, accessed August 12, 2023, https://bureauoflinguisticalreality.com/portfolio/psychic-corpus-dissonance/.
12 "Psychic Corpus Dissonance," Bureau of Linguistical Reality.
13 Glenn Albrecht, *Earth Emotions: New Words for a New World* (Ithaca, NY: Cornell University Press, 2019), 38–39.
14 Albrecht, *Earth Emotions*, 199–201.

15 See Victoria Loorz's website (https://www.victorialoorz.com/eco-spiritual-direction), which describes her ecospiritual direction program and her book *Church of the Wild: How Nature Invites Us into the Sacred* (Minneapolis: Broadleaf Books, 2021) for an introduction to important transformations open to community gatherings.
16 Ecotherapeutic writings inform what I suggest here as possibilities. See Caroline Brazier, *Ecotherapy in Practice: A Buddhist Model* (New York: Routledge, 2018); Linda Buzzell and Craig Chalquist, eds., *Ecotherapy: Healing with Nature in Mind* (Berkeley, CA: Counterpoint, 2009); Nick Totten, *Wild Therapy: Rewilding Our Inner and Outer Worlds* (Monmouth, UK: PCCS Books, 2021); Martin Jordan and Joe Hinds, eds., *Ecotherapy: Theory, Research and Practice* (New York: Palgrave Macmillan, 2016).
17 John Wortley, trans. *The Book of the Elders: Sayings of the Desert Fathers* (Collegeville, MN: Liturgical Press, 2012), 22.
18 Wortley, *The Book of the Elders*, 321.
19 Emily Wall, "This Forest, This Beach, You," Alaska Center for the Book, Poems in Place Art Installation (Totem Bight, AK, 2013). www.alaskacenterforthebook.org/poems-in-place-photo-gallery/.

CHAPTER 3

1 Martin Shaw, "Navigating the Mysteries," *Emergence Magazine* 3 (2022): 29.
2 Berry, *The Christian Future*, 8–9.
3 Thomas Merton, *New Seeds of Contemplation* (Boston: Shambhala, 2003), 31.
4 Haraway, *Staying with the Trouble*, 127.
5 Cláudio Carvalhaes, *Ritual at World's End: Essays on Eco-Liturgical Liberation Theology* (York, PA: Barber's Son Press, 2021), 248–49.
6 Columba Stewart, "The Greening of Asceticism," *The Way* 31, no. 4 (1991): 303.
7 Stewart, "The Greening of Asceticism," 309.
8 Francis, *Laudate Deum*, Apostolic Exhortation of the Holy Father: To All People of Good Will on the Climate Crisis, October 4, 2023, paragraph 59. https://www.vatican.va/content/francesco/en/apost_exhortations/documents/20231004-laudate-deum.html.
9 David G. R. Keller, *Oasis of Wisdom: The Worlds of the Desert Fathers and Mothers* (Collegeville, MN: Liturgical Press, 2005), 48.
10 See Elizabeth O'Donnell Gandalfo, *Ecomartyrdom in the Americas: Living and Dying for Our Common Home* (Maryknoll, NY: Orbis Books, 2023).
11 Stewart, "The Greening of Asceticism," 308–09.
12 Benedicta Ward, trans. *The Sayings of the Desert Fathers: The Alphabetical Collection*, rev. ed. (Kalamazoo, MI: Cistercian Publications, 1984), 103.
13 Rachel Wheeler, *Desert Daughters, Desert Sons: Rethinking the Christian Desert Tradition* (Collegeville, MN: Liturgical Press, 2020).

14 John Wortley, ed. *More Sayings of the Desert Fathers: An English Translation and Notes* (New York: Cambridge University Press, 2019), 120.
15 John Wortley, ed. *The Anonymous Sayings of the Desert Fathers: A Select Edition and Complete English Translation* (Cambridge: Cambridge University Press, 2013), 349–51. Another, shorter version (p. 55) links the desert Christian with antelope companions whom he leaves, similarly to how this story begins, but it eliminates the section detailing the man becoming trapped.
16 Alexis Pauline Gumbs, *Undrowned: Black Feminist Lessons from Marine Mammals* (Chico, CA: AK Press, 2020), 44. Italics mine.
17 See Paula and Macrina, for example. Their stories are told in Joan M. Petersen, trans., *Handmaids of the Lord: Holy Women in Late Antiquity and the Early Middle Ages* (Kalamazoo, MI: Cistercian Publications, 1996).
18 Marjorie J. Thompson, *Soul Feast: An Invitation to the Christian Spiritual Life*, newly rev. ed. (Louisville: Westminster John Knox Press, 2014), 149.
19 Gertrude the Great of Helfta, *Spiritual Exercises*, trans. Gertrud Jaron Lewis and Jack Lewis (Kalamazoo, MI: Cistercian Publications, 1989), 145.
20 "The Life of Melangell," in *Celtic Christian Spirituality: An Anthology of Medieval and Modern Sources*, ed. Oliver Davies and Fiona Bowie (New York: Continuum, 1995), 65–67.
21 Caroline Malim, "As Above, So Below: St. Melangell and the Celestial Journey," in *Lands of the Shamans: Archaeology, Landscape and Cosmology*, ed. Dragos Gheorghiu, George Nash, Herman Bender, and Emilia Pasztor (Oxford: Oxbow Books, 2018), 98.
22 *Grist*, "Imagine 2200," https://grist.org/fix/series/imagine-2200-climate-fiction/.
23 Robin Wall Kimmerer, *Braiding Sweetgrass: Indigenous Wisdom, Scientific Knowledge, and the Teaching of Plants* (Minneapolis: Milkweed Editions, 2013), 37.
24 Kimmerer, *Braiding Sweetgrass*, 37.
25 Francis Weller, *The Wild Edge of Sorrow: Rituals of Renewal and the Sacred Work of Grief* (Berkeley, CA: North Atlantic Books, 2015), 76.
26 Carvalhaes, *Ritual at World's End*, 22.
27 Craig Chalquist, *Terrapsychological Inquiry: Restorying Our Relationship with Nature, Place, and Planet* (New York: Routledge, 2020), 26–27.

CHAPTER 4

1 Christena Cleveland, *God Is a Black Woman* (New York: Amistad, 2022), 98 and 103.
2 Stephen D. Moore, ed., *Divinanimality: Animal Theory, Creaturely Theology* (New York: Fordham University Press, 2014).
3 Daphne Hampson, *After Christianity* (Valley Forge, PA: Trinity Press, 1996), 10.

4 David Abram, *Becoming Animal: An Earthly Cosmology* (New York: Vintage Books, 2010), 278.
5 Haraway, *Staying with the Trouble*, 131.
6 Evagrius Ponticus, *Chapters on Prayer*, trans. John Eudes Bamberger (Collegeville, MN: Cistercian Publications, 1972), 65.
7 Francis, *Laudato Si'*, Encyclical Letter of the Holy Father: On Care for Our Common Home, May 24, 2015, paragraph 222, 2015, https://www.vatican.va/content/francesco/en/encyclicals/documents/papa-francesco_20150524_enciclica-laudato-si.html.
8 McFague, *Super, Nature Christians*, 174.
9 Macrina Wiederkehr, *Seasons of Your Heart: Prayers and Reflections* (New York: HarperCollins, 1991), 5. Italics mine.
10 Mark Hathaway and Leonardo Boff, *The Tao of Liberation: Exploring the Ecology of Transformation* (Maryknoll, NY: Orbis Book, 2009), 329.
11 Tim Robinson, *Setting Foot on the Shores of Connemara*. Dublin: Lilliput, 1996.
12 Sallie McFague, *Models of God: Theology for an Ecological, Nuclear Age* (Philadelphia: Fortress Press, 1987), 69–78.
13 Thomas Keating, *Open Mind, Open Heart: The Contemplative Dimension of the Gospel* (New York: Continuum, 2003), 63.
14 Wortley, *The Book of the Elders*, 146.
15 This story can be found in the tenth conference ("On Prayer") in John Cassian's *Conferences*, trans. Boniface Ramsey, OP (New York: Newman Press, 1997), 372–73.
16 Cleveland, *God Is a Black Woman*.
17 SAID, *99 Psalms*, trans. Mark S. Burrows (Brewster, MA: Paraclete Press, 2013), 87.
18 See Andrea M. Couture, "Creating a Sense of Reverence for Every Species," *Sojourners* (July 2022).

CHAPTER 5

1 Kim Stafford, "Citizen of Dark Times," in *Wild Honey, Tough Salt: Poems* (Pasadena, CA: Red Hen Press, 2019), 44.
2 Suzanne Simard, *Finding the Mother Tree: Discovering the Wisdom of the Forest* (New York: Vintage Books, 2022), 183.
3 Holten, ed, *The Language of Trees*. A snippet of Holten's collaboration with Forrest Gander is available at https://emergencemagazine.org/feature/forest/.
4 Francis, *Evangelii Gaudium*, Apostolic Exhortation of the Holy Father: To the Bishops, Clergy, Consecrated Persons and the Lay Faithful on the Proclamation of the Gospel in Today's World, November 24, 2013, paragraph 215, https://www.vatican.va/content/francesco/en/apost_exhortations/

documents/papa-francesco_esortazione-ap_20131124_evangelii-gaudium.html. Repeated in *Laudato Si'*, paragraph 89.

5 Carl Phillips, "Among the Trees," in Holten, ed., *The Language of Trees*, 150–51.

6 My practice in using nongendered pronouns for Earth creatures is informed by Robin Wall Kimmerer's suggestions of ki (singular) and kin (plural) in "Nature Needs a New Pronoun: To Stop the Age of Extinction, Let's Start by Ditching 'It,'" *Yes!* (March 30, 2015). https://www.yesmagazine.org/issue/together-earth/2015/03/30/alternative-grammar-a-new-language-of-kinship.

7 Steven Chase, *Nature as Spiritual Practice* (Grand Rapids, MI: Eerdmans, 2011), 125–60.

8 Enrique Salmón, "Connection to the Land," in *Restoring the Kinship Worldview: Indigenous Voices Introduce 28 Precepts for Rebalancing Life on Planet Earth*, ed. Wahinkpe Topa and Darcia Narvaez (Berkeley, CA: North Atlantic Books, 2022), 219–27.

9 Denise Levertov, "The Wound," in *Sands of the Well* (New York: New Directions, 1996), 7.

10 Ramón Grosfoguel, "The Structure of Knowledge in Westernized Universities: Epistemic Racism/Sexism and the Four Genocides/Epistemicides of the Long 16th Century," *Human Architecture: Journal of the Sociology of Self-Knowledge* 11, no. 1 (Fall 2013): 73–90.

CHAPTER 6

1 Robin Wall Kimmerer, "Building Good Soil," in *What Kind of Ancestor Do You Want to Be?*, ed. John Hausdoerffer, Brooke Parry Hecht, Melissa K. Nelson, and Katherine Kassouf Cummings (Chicago: University of Chicago Press, 2021). Also cited in an interview with Kimmerer in Andrew Boyd, *I Want a Better Catastrophe: Navigating the Climate Crisis with Grief, Hope, and Gallows Humor* (Gabriola Island, BC: New Society Publishers, 2023), 297.

2 Kimmerer, *Braiding Sweetgrass*, 123.

3 Wortley, *The Book of the Elders*, 104.

4 Athanasius, *The Life of Antony*, 68; Jerome, "The Life of St. Paul the First Hermit," in *The Desert Fathers*, trans. Helen Waddell (New York: Vintage Books, 1998), 36.

5 Chellis Glendinning's phrase. See *My Name is Chellis and I'm in Recovery from Western Civilization* (Gabriola Island, BC: New Catalyst Books, 2007), 57–68.

6 Anders Nygren, *Agape and Eros* (Chicago: University of Chicago Press, 1982), 75–80.

7 Wortley, *More Sayings of the Desert Fathers*, 119.

8 Wortley, *More Sayings of the Desert Fathers*, 130 and 135.

9 Lao-Tzu, *Tao Te Ching*, trans. Stephen Mitchell (New York: Harper Perennial, 2006), section 22.
10 Weller, *The Wild Edge of Sorrow*, 47.
11 Trebbe Johnson, *Radical Joy for Hard Times: Finding Meaning and Making Beauty in Earth's Broken Places* (Berkeley, CA: North Atlantic Books, 2018), 151.

CHAPTER 7

1 Haraway, *Staying with the Trouble*, 126.
2 Loorz, *Church of the Wild*, 169–188.
3 See Robert D. Romanyshyn, *The Wounded Researcher: Research with Soul in Mind* (New Orleans: Spring Journal Books, 2013).
4 Manish Jain and Kalashree Sengupta, "The Journey to Alivelihoods," *Medium* (July 1, 2023), https://medium.com/ecoversities-alliance/the-journey-to-alivelihoods-6f0465cac248.
5 Joanna Macy and Chris Johnston, *Active Hope: How to Face the Mess We're in with Unexpected Resilience and Creative Power* (Novato: New World Library, 2022), 26–33.
6 Francis, *Laudato Si'*, paragraphs 216–21.
7 Francis, *Laudato Si'*, paragraphs 2, 49, and 53.
8 Macy and Johnston, *Active Hope*, 26.
9 Boyd, *I Want a Better Catastrophe.*
10 Wortley, *The Book of the Elders*, 33.
11 Haraway, *Staying*, 32.
12 Wortley, *The Book of the Elders*, 11.
13 A favorite aligned resource from the work of ecotherapists is Linda Buzzell and Craig Chalquist's "Twenty Principles of Ecoresilience: Personal and Cultural Adaptation to a Changed Planet," *Communities* 174 (Spring 2017): 51–73.
14 David Holmgren, *Permaculture: Principles and Pathways Beyond Sustainability* (Hepburn, Australia: Holmgren Design Services, 2002).
15 adrienne maree brown, *Emergent Strategy: Shaping Change, Changing Worlds* (Chico, CA: AK Press, 2017), 41.
16 A podcast series title as well as subject of his reflections, dated January 6, 2017, available at https://www.bayoakomolafe.net/post/the-edges-in-the-middle.
17 Andrew Boyd, "Interview with Gopal Dayaneni," in *I Want a Better Catastrophe*, 140–41.
18 Wortley, *The Book of the Elders*, 365.
19 Kim Stafford, "Proclamation for Peace," in *Wild Honey, Tough Salt: Poems* (Pasadena, CA: Red Hen Press, 2019), 54.

EPILOGUE

1 Denise Levertov, "Beginners," in *The Collected Poems of Denise Levertov*, ed. Paul A. Lacey and Anne Dewey (New York: New Directions, 2013), 653–54.

Bibliography

Abram, David. *Becoming Animal: An Earthly Cosmology*. New York: Vintage Books, 2010.

———. *The Spell of the Sensuous: Perception and Language in a More-Than-Human World*. New York: Pantheon Books, 1996.

Alaimo, Stacy. *Bodily Natures: Science, Environment, and the Material Self*. Bloomington: Indiana University Press, 2010.

———. *Exposed: Environmental Politics and Pleasures in Posthuman Times*. Minneapolis: University of Minnesota Press, 2016.

Albrecht, Glenn. *Earth Emotions: New Words for a New World*. Ithaca, NY: Cornell University Press, 2019.

Arendt, Hannah. *The Origins of Totalitarianism*. New York: Harvest, 1973.

Athanasius. *The Life of Antony*. Translated by Robert C. Gregg. New York: Paulist Press, 1980.

Berry, Thomas. *The Christian Future and the Fate of Earth*. Maryknoll, NY: Orbis Books, 2009.

———. *The Dream of the Earth*. San Francisco: Sierra Club Books, 1990.

———. *The Great Work: Our Way into the Future*. New York: Harmony/Bell Tower, 1999.

Boyd, Andrew. *I Want a Better Catastrophe: Navigating the Climate Crisis with Grief, Hope, and Gallows Humor*. Gabriola Island, BC: New Society Publishers, 2023.

Brazier, Caroline. *Ecotherapy in Practice: A Buddhist Model*. New York: Routledge, 2018.

brown, adrienne maree. *Emergent Strategy: Shaping Change, Changing Worlds.* Chico, CA: AK Press, 2017.

Bureau of Linguistical Reality. https://bureauoflinguisticalreality.com.

Buzzell, Linda, and Craig Chalquist, eds. *Ecotherapy: Healing with Nature in Mind.* Berkeley, CA: Counterpoint, 2009.

———. "Twenty Principles of Ecoresilience: Personal and Cultural Adaptation to a Changed Planet." *Communities* 174 (Spring 2017): 51–73.

Canty, Jeanine M. *Returning the Self to Nature: Undoing Our Collective Narcissism and Healing Our Planet.* Boulder: Shambhala, 2022.

Carvalhaes, Cláudio. *Ritual at World's End: Essays on Eco-Liturgical Liberation Theology.* York, PA: Barber's Son Press, 2021.

Chalquist, Craig. *Terrapsychological Inquiry: Restorying Our Relationship with Nature, Place, and Planet.* New York: Routledge, 2020.

Chase, Steven. *Nature as Spiritual Practice.* Grand Rapids: Eerdmans, 2011.

Christie, Douglas E. *The Blue Sapphire of the Mind: Notes for a Contemplative Ecology.* New York: Oxford University Press, 2013.

Cleveland, Christena. *God Is a Black Woman.* New York: Amistad, 2022.

Couture, Andrea M. "Creating a Sense of Reverence for Every Species." *Sojourners* (July 2022). https://sojo.net/magazine/july-2022/creating-sense-reverence-every-species.

Dahill, Lisa. "Into Local Waters: Rewilding the Study of Christian Spirituality." *Spiritus* 16, no. 2 (Fall 2016): 141–65.

Davies, Oliver, and Fiona Bowie, eds. *Celtic Christian Spirituality: An Anthology of Medieval and Modern Sources.* New York: Continuum, 1995.

Eucherius of Lyon. "In Praise of the Desert." Translated by Charles Cummings. In *The Lives of the Jura Fathers*, edited by Tim Vivian, Kim Vivian, and Jeffrey Burton Russell, 197–215. Kalamazoo, MI: Cistercian Publications, 1999.

Evagrius Ponticus. *The Praktikos and Chapters on Prayer.* Translated by John Eudes Bamberger. Collegeville, MN: Cistercian Publications, 1972.

Francis. Evangelii Gaudium. Apostolic Exhortation of the Holy Father: To the Bishops, Clergy, Consecrated Persons and the Lay Faithful on the Proclamation of the Gospel in Today's World. November 24, 2013. https://www.vatican.va/content/francesco/en/apost_exhortations/documents/papa-francesco_esortazione-ap_20131124_evangelii-gaudium.html.

———.Laudate Deum. Apostolic Exhortation of the Holy Father: To All People of Good Will on the Climate Crisis. October 4, 2023. https://www.vatican.va/content/francesco/en/apost_exhortations/documents/20231004-laudate-deum.html.

———.Laudato Si'. Encyclical Letter of the Holy Father: On Care for Our Common Home. May 24, 2015. https://www.vatican.va/content/francesco/en/encyclicals/documents/papa-francesco_20150524_enciclica-laudato-si.html.

Gandalfo, Elizabeth O'Donnell. *Ecomartyrdom in the Americas: Living and Dying for Our Common Home.* Maryknoll, NY: Orbis Books, 2023.

Gertrude the Great of Helfta. *Spiritual Exercises.* Translated by Gertrud Jaron Lewis and Jack Lewis. Kalamazoo, MI: Cistercian Publications, 1989.

Glendinning, Chellis. *My Name is Chellis and I'm in Recovery from Western Civilization.* Gabriola Island, BC: New Catalyst Books, 2007.

Grist. "Imagine 2200." https://grist.org/fix/series/imagine-2200-climate-fiction/.

Grosfoguel, Ramón. "The Structure of Knowledge in Westernized Universities: Epistemic Racism/Sexism and the Four Genocides/Epistemicides of the Long 16th Century." *Human Architecture: Journal of the Sociology of Self-Knowledge* 11, no. 1 (Fall 2013): 73–90.

Gumbs, Alexis Pauline. *Undrowned: Black Feminist Lessons from Marine Mammals.* Chico, CA: AK Press, 2020.

Habel, Norman. *An Inconvenient Text: Is a Green Reading of the Bible Possible?* Adelaide: ATF Press, 2009.

Hampson, Daphne. *After Christianity.* Valley Forge, PA: Trinity Press, 1996.

Haraway, Donna. *Staying with the Trouble: Making Kin in the Chthulucene.* Durham, NC: Duke University Press, 2016.

Hathaway, Mark, and Leonardo Boff. *The Tao of Liberation: Exploring the Ecology of Transformation.* Maryknoll, NY: Orbis Books, 2009.

Hinton, David. *Desert: Poems.* Boulder: Shambhala, 2018.

Holmgren, David. *Permaculture: Principles and Pathways beyond Sustainability.* Hepburn, Australia: Holmgren Design Services, 2002.

Holten, Katie, ed. *The Language of Trees: A Rewilding of Literature and Landscape.* Portland, OR: Tin House, 2023.

Isasi-Díaz, Ada María. *Mujerista Theology: A Theology for the Twenty-First Century.* Maryknoll, NY: Orbis Books, 1996.

Jain, Manish, and Kalashree Sengupta. "The Journey to Alivelihoods." *Medium* (July 1, 2023). https://medium.com/ecoversities-alliance/the-journey-to-alivelihoods-6f0465cac248.

Jerome. "The Life of St. Paul the First Hermit." In *The Desert Fathers,* translated by Helen Waddell, 34–43. New York: Vintage Books, 1998.

John Cassian. *Conferences.* Translated by Boniface Ramsey. New York: Newman Press, 1997.

John Moschos. *The Spiritual Meadow.* Translated by John Wortley. Kalamazoo, MI: Cistercian Publications, 1992.

Johnson, Trebbe. *Radical Joy for Hard Times: Finding Meaning and Making Beauty in Earth's Broken Places.* Berkeley, CA: North Atlantic Books, 2018.

Jordan, Martin, and Joe Hinds, eds. *Ecotherapy: Theory, Research and Practice.* New York: Palgrave Macmillan, 2016.

Jung, Carl Gustav. *The Earth Has a Soul: C. G. Jung on Nature, Technology and Modern Life.* Edited by Meredith Sabini. Berkeley, CA: North Atlantic Books, 2008.

Keating, Thomas. *Open Mind, Open Heart: The Contemplative Dimension of the Gospel*. New York: Continuum, 2003.

Keller, David G. R. *Oasis of Wisdom: The Worlds of the Desert Fathers and Mothers*. Collegeville, MN: Liturgical Press, 2005.

Kimmerer, Robin Wall. *Braiding Sweetgrass: Indigenous Wisdom, Scientific Knowledge, and the Teaching of Plants*. Minneapolis: Milkwood Editions, 2013.

———. "Building Good Soil." In *What Kind of Ancestor Do You Want to Be?*, edited by John Hausdoerffer, Brooke Parry Hecht, Melissa K. Nelson, and Katherine Kassouf Cummings, 182–84. Chicago: University of Chicago Press, 2021.

———. "Nature Needs a New Pronoun: To Stop the Age of Extinction, Let's Start by Ditching 'It.'" *Yes!* (March 30, 2015). https://www.yesmagazine.org/issue/together-earth/2015/03/30/alternative-grammar-a-new-language-of-kinship.

———. "Speaking of Nature." *Orion Magazine* (2017). https://orionmagazine.org/article/speaking-of-nature/.

Lao-Tzu. *Tao Te Ching*. Translated by Stephen Mitchell. New York: Harper Perennial, 2006.

Lauck, Joanne. *The Voice of the Infinite in the Small: Re-envisioning the Insect-Human Connection*. Boston: Shambhala, 2002.

Levertov, Denise. *The Collected Poems of Denise Levertov*. Edited by Paul A. Lacey and Anne Dewey. New York: New Directions, 2013.

Levertov, Denise. *Sands of the Well*. New York: New Directions, 1996.

Lipsitz, George. "Foreword: Accompaniment as a Way of Life." In *Mutual Accompaniment and the Creation of the Commons*, by Mary Watkins, xi–xv. New Haven: Yale University Press, 2019.

Loorz, Victoria. *Church of the Wild: How Nature Invites Us into the Sacred*. Minneapolis: Broadleaf Books, 2021.

Louv, Richard. *Last Child in the Woods: Saving Our Children from Nature-Deficit Disorder*. Chapel Hill, NC: Algonquin Books, 2005.

———. *Our Wild Calling: How Connecting with Animals Can Transform Our Lives—and Save Theirs*. Chapel Hill, NC: Algonquin Books, 2019.

———. *Vitamin N: The Essential Guide to a Nature-Rich Life*. Chapel Hill, NC: Algonquin Books, 2016.

Machado de Oliveira, Vanessa. *Hospicing Modernity: Facing Humanity's Wrongs and the Implications for Social Activism*. Berkeley, CA: North Atlantic Books, 2021.

Macy, Joanna, and Chris Johnston. *Active Hope: How to Face the Mess We're in with Unexpected Resilience and Creative Power*. Novato, CA: New World Library, 2022.

Malim, Caroline. "As Above, So Below: St. Melangell and the Celestial Journey." In *Lands of the Shamans: Archaeology, Landscape and Cosmology*, edited by Dragos Ghorghiu, George Nash, Herman Bender, and Emilia Pasztor, 89–110. Oxford: Oxbow Books, 2018.

Mathews, Freya. "Burning Our Kin." In *Persons*, edited by Gavin Van Horn, Robin Wall Kimmerer, and John Hausdoerffer, 93-102. Vol. 4 of *Kinship: Belonging in a World of Relations*. Libertyville, IL: Center for Humans and Nature Press, 2021.

McFague, Sallie. *Models of God: Theology for an Ecological, Nuclear Age*. Philadelphia: Fortress Press, 1987.

———. *Super, Natural Christians: How We Should Love Nature*. Minneapolis: Fortress Press, 1997.

McGinnis, Michael V. "Myth, Nature, and the Bureaucratic Experience." *Environmental Ethics* 16, no. 4 (1994): 425–36.

Merton, Thomas. *New Seeds of Contemplation*. Boston: Shambhala, 2003.

———. *A Search for Solitude: Pursuing the Monk's True Life*. Edited by Lawrence S. Cunningham. New York: HarperCollins, 1997.

Meyer, Eric Daryl. *Inner Animalities: Theology and the End of the Human*. New York: Fordham University Press, 2018.

Moore, Stephen D., ed. *Divinanimality: Animal Theory, Creaturely Theology*. New York: Fordham University Press, 2014.

Nygren, Anders. *Agape and Eros*. Chicago: University of Chicago Press, 1982.

O'Donohue, John. *To Bless the Space between Us: A Book of Blessings*. New York: Convergent Books, 2008.

Penniman, Leah. *Black Earth Wisdom: Soulful Conversations with Black Environmentalists*. New York: Amistad, 2023.

Petersen, Joan M., ed. *Handmaids of the Lord: Holy Women in Late Antiquity and the Early Middle Ages*. Kalamazoo, MI: Cistercian Publications, 1996.

Phillips, Carl. "Among the Trees." In *The Language of Trees: A Rewilding of Literature and Landscape*, edited by Katie Holten, 149–56. Portland, OR: Tin House Books, 2023.

Plumwood, Val. *The Eye of the Crocodile*. Canberra: Australian National University E Press, 2012.

Pyle, Robert. *The Thunder Tree: Lessons from an Urban Wildland*. Boston: Houghton Mifflin, 1993.

Robinson, Tim. *Setting Foot on the Shores of Connemara*. Dublin: Lilliput, 1996.

Romanyshyn, Robert D. *The Wounded Researcher: Research with Soul in Mind*. New Orleans: Spring Journal Books, 2013.

SAID. *99 Psalms*. Translated by Mark S. Burrows. Brewster, MA: Paraclete Press, 2013.

Salmón, Enrique. "Connection to the Land." In *Restoring the Kinship Worldview: Indigenous Voices Introduce 28 Precepts for Rebalancing Life on Planet Earth*, edited by Wahinkpe Topa and Darcia Narvaez, 219–27. Berkeley, CA: North Atlantic Books, 2022.

Schneiders, Sandra M. "The Study of Christian Spirituality: Contours and Dynamics of a Discipline." In *Minding the Spirit: The Study of Christian Spirituality*, edited by Elizabeth A. Dreyer and Mark S. Burrows, 5–24. Baltimore: Johns Hopkins University Press, 2005.

Shaw, Martin. "Navigating the Mysteries." *Emergence Magazine* 3 (2022): 27–30.

Simard, Suzanne. *Finding the Mother Tree: Discovering the Wisdom of the Forest*. New York: Vintage Books, 2022.

Stafford, Kim. *Wild Honey, Tough Salt: Poems*. Pasadena, CA: Red Hen Press, 2019.

Stewart, Columba. "The Greening of Asceticism." *The Way* 31, no. 4 (1991): 303–12.

Thompson, Marjorie J. *Soul Feast: An Invitation to the Christian Spiritual Life*. Newly Revised Edition. Louisville: Westminster John Knox Press, 2014.

Thunberg, Greta. "Speech at the U.N. Climate Action Summit." September 23, 2019. https://www.npr.org/2019/09/23/763452863/transcript-greta-thunbergs-speech-at-the-u-n-climate-action-summit.

Totten, Nick. *Wild Therapy: Rewilding Our Inner and Outer Worlds*. Monmouth, UK: PCCS Books, 2021.

Wall, Emily. "This Forest, This Beach, You." Alaska Center for the Book, Poems in Place Art Installation. Totem Bight, AK, 2013.

Ward, Benedicta, trans. *The Sayings of the Desert Fathers: The Alphabetical Collection*. Revised Edition. Kalamazoo, MI: Cistercian Publications, 1984.

Weller, Francis. *The Wild Edge of Sorrow: Rituals of Renewal and the Sacred Work of Grief*. Berkeley, CA: North Atlantic Books, 2015.

Wheeler, Rachel. *Desert Daughters, Desert Sons: Rethinking the Christian Desert Tradition*. Collegeville, MN: Liturgical Press, 2020.

White, Lynn, Jr. "The Historical Roots of our Ecologic Crisis." *Science* 155 (1967): 1203–07.

Wiederkehr, Macrina. *Seasons of Your Heart: Prayers and Reflections*. New York: HarperCollins, 1991.

Wilson, Edward O. *Half Earth: Our Planet's Fight for Life*. New York: Liveright, 2016.

Wortley, John, trans. *The Anonymous Sayings of the Desert Fathers: A Select Edition and Complete English Translation*. Cambridge: Cambridge University Press, 2013.

———, trans. *The Book of the Elders: Sayings of the Desert Fathers: The Systematic Collection*. Cistercian Studies 240. Collegeville, MN: Liturgical Press, 2012.

———, trans. *More Sayings of the Desert Fathers: An English Translation and Notes*. New York: Cambridge University Press, 2019.

Index